BCN *free* ART

01

The Port and Barceloneta

Other BCN *free* ART routes

More free art in Barcelona at
www.barcelonafreeart.net

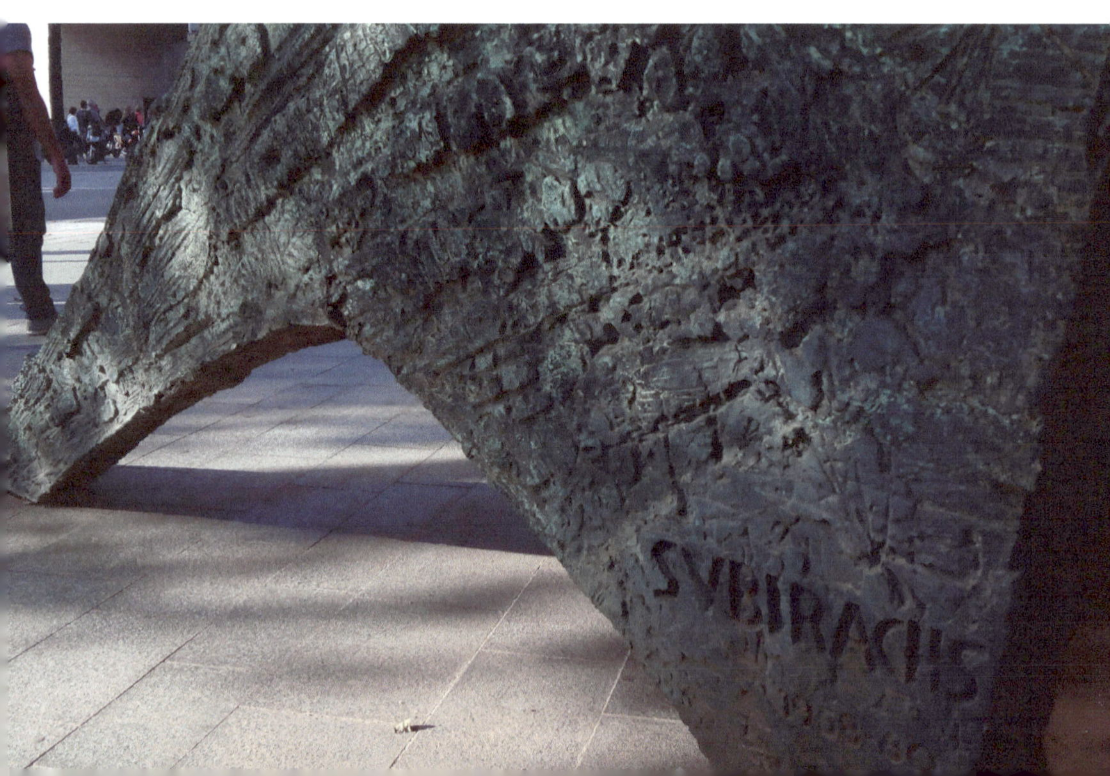

BCN *free* ART 01

The Port and Barceloneta

A guide to free art in Barcelona

Kevin Booth

POBLESECBOOKS

Published by Poble Sec Books in 2016. First edition.

Printed in the United Kingdom by Lightning Source UK Ltd.

ISBN: 978-0-9932298-1-7 (.epub) / 978-0-9932298-0-0 (print)

British Library Cataloguing in Publication Data.
A CIP catalogue record for this book is available from the British Library.

www.poblesecbooks.com

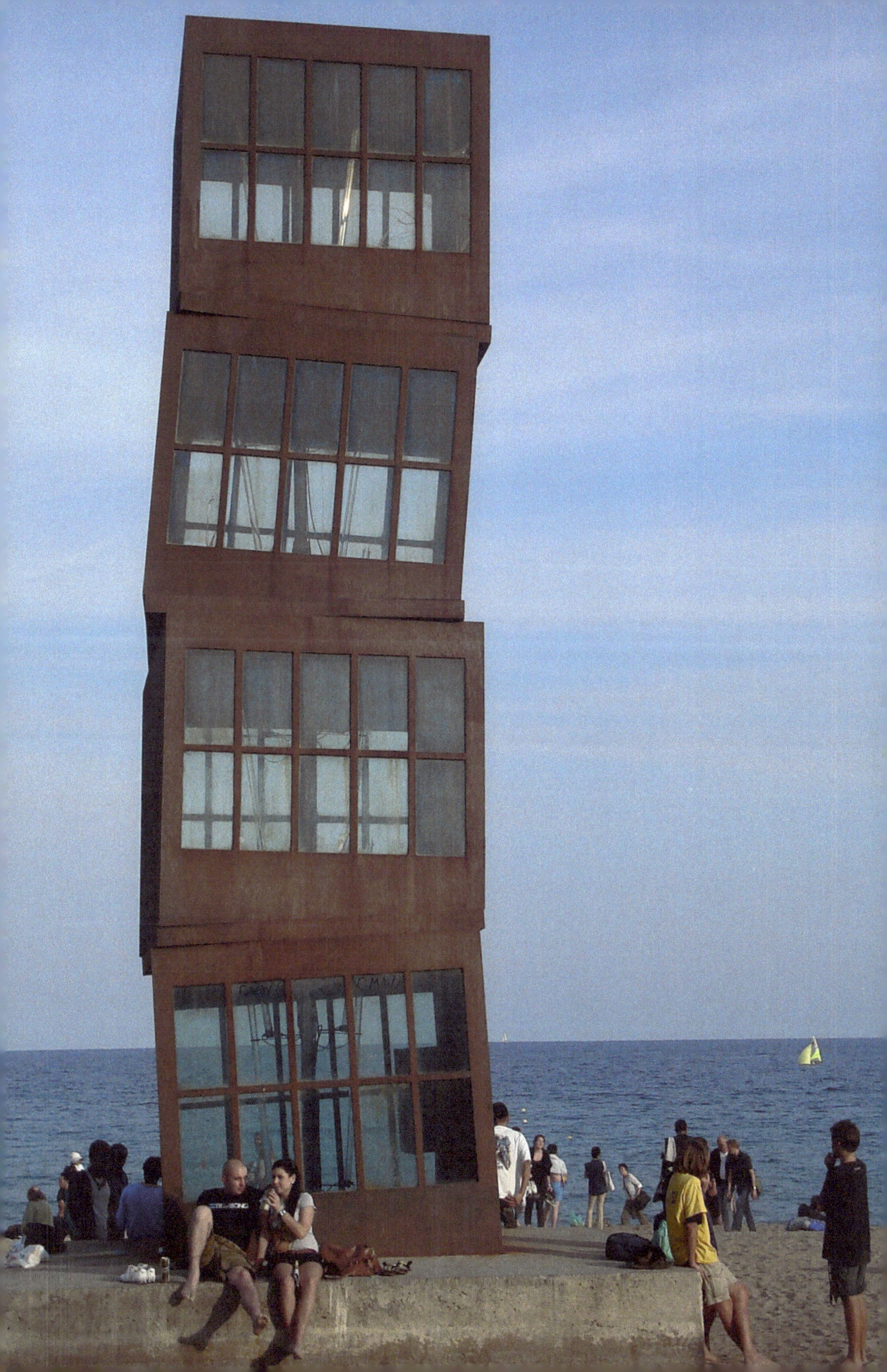

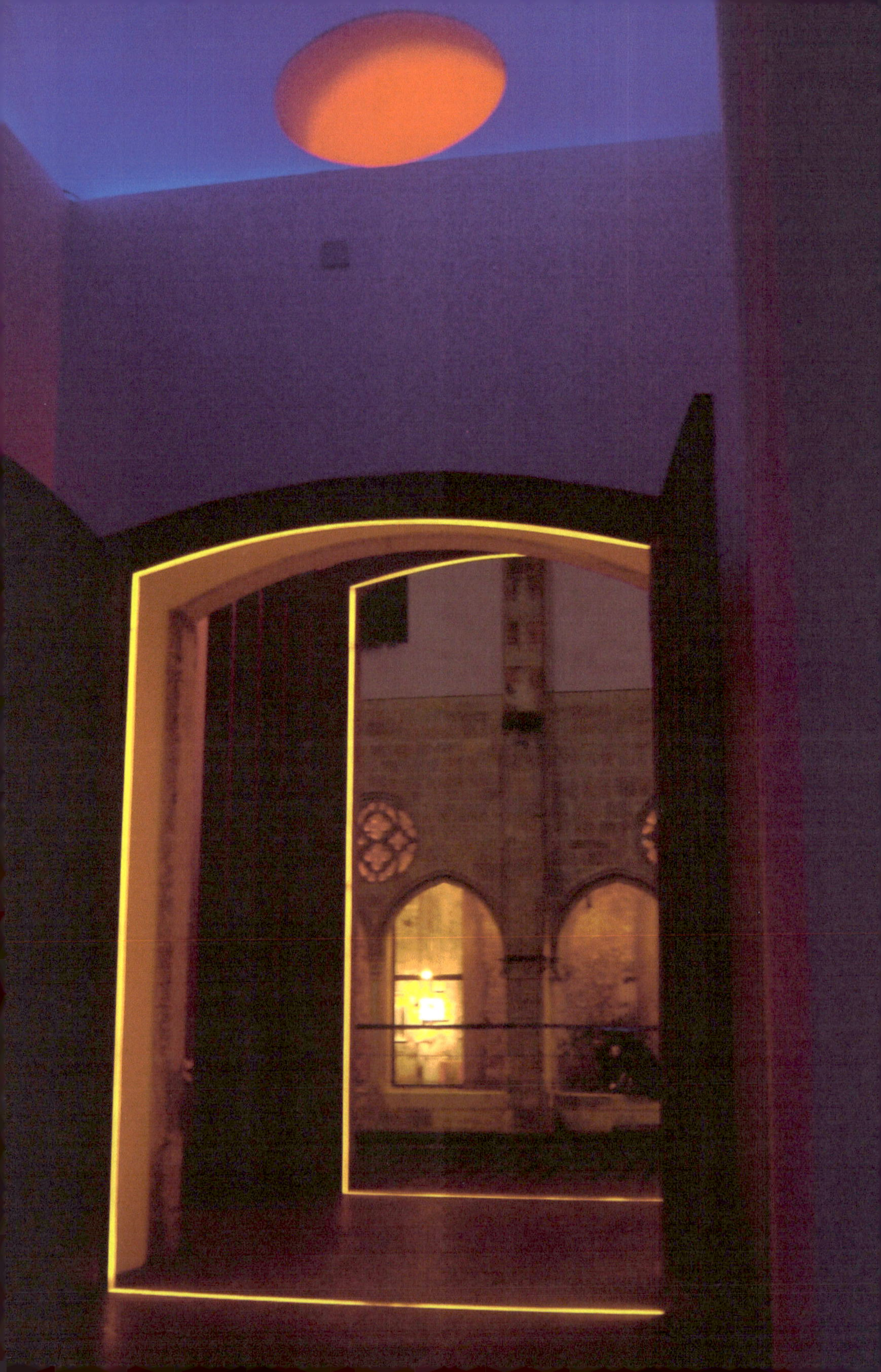

CONTENTS

The Port and Barceloneta —sites of the artworks

Key:

01. *Monument to Columbus* (1885), Gaietà Buïgas i Monravà *et al.*

02. *Stargazers* (2006), Robert Llimós.

03. *To Joan Salvat Papasseit* (1992), Robert Krier.

04. *The Couple* (1998), Lautaro Díaz Silva.

05. *Gambrinus* (1989), Xavier Mariscal.

06. *Barcelona's Head* (1992), Roy Lichtenstein & Diego Delgado Rajado.

UC01. *Deuce Coop* (1992*), James Turrell.

UC02. *Born* (1992*), Jaume Plensa.

UC03. *Untitled (Four Wedges)* (1992*), Ulrich Rückriem.

07. *Compass Rose* (1992*), Lothar Baumgarten.

08. *Growing in Appearance* (1992*), Mario Merz.

09. *Evocation of Seafaring* (1958–1960), X. Subirachs.

10. *A Room Where It Is Always Raining* (1992*), Juan Muñoz.

11. *The Wounded Star* (1992*), Rebecca Horn.

12. *Roman Scales* (1993*), Jannis Kounellis.

13. Catalana de Gas water tower (1907), Josep Domènech i Estapà.

*Works in the permanent outdoor exhibition "Urban Configurations", 1992.

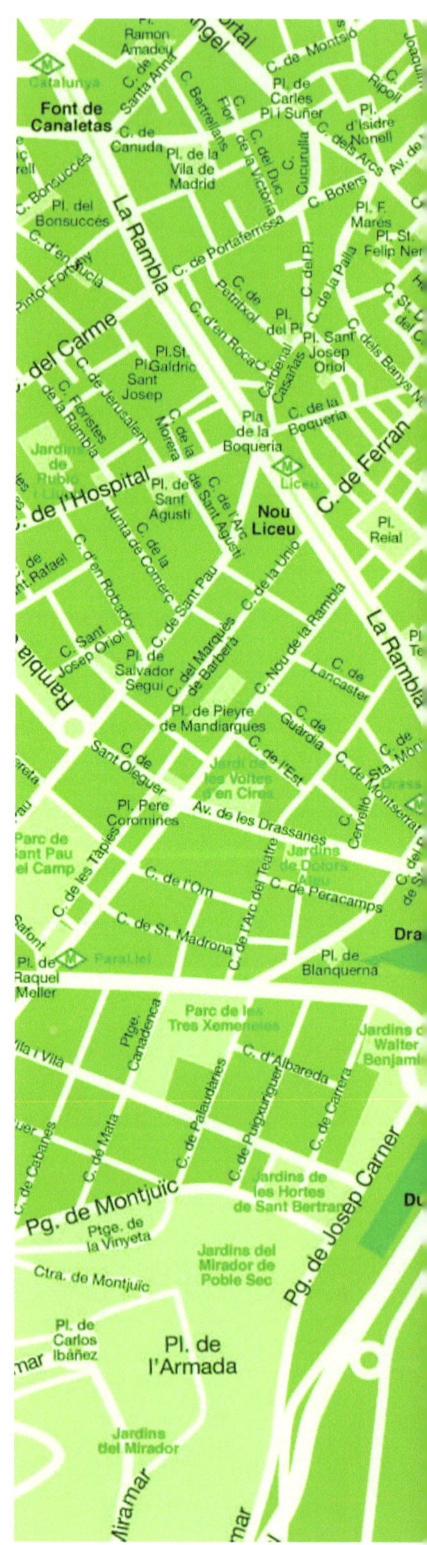

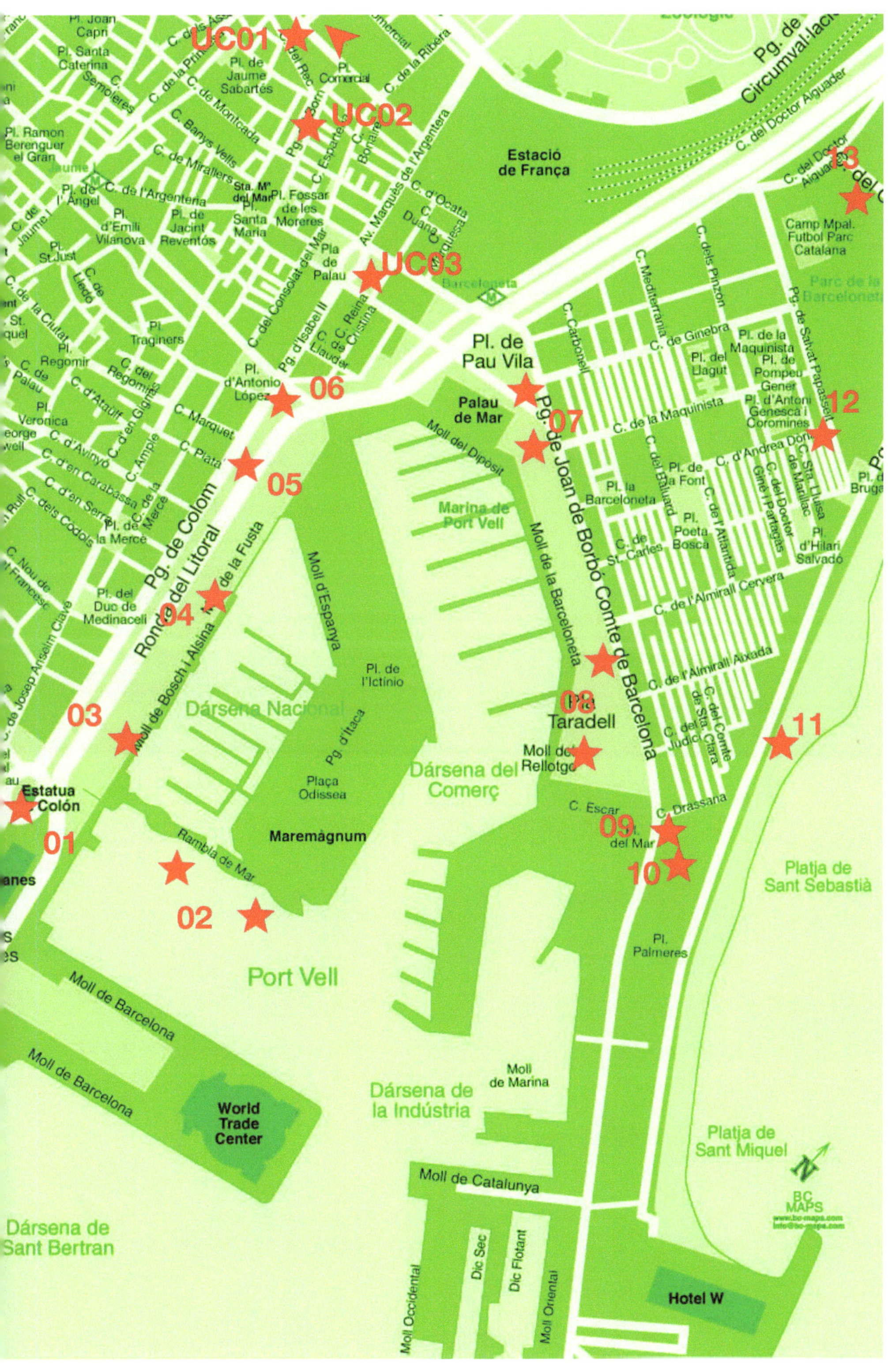

UC01
UC02
UC03
01
02
03
04
05
06
07
08
09
10
11
12
13
Pl. Joan Capri
Pl. Santa Caterina
Semoleres
C. dels Assaonadors
Pl. de Jaume Sabartés
C. de la Princesa
Pl. Comercial
C. del Rec
C. de la Ribera
Pg. de Circumval·lació
Pl. Ramon Berenguer el Gran
C. de Montcada
C. Banys Vells
C. de Miralles
C. Esparteria
C. Bonaire
C. de Cremat
C. Marquès de l'Argentera
Estació de França
C. del Doctor Aiguader
C. del Doctor Aiguader
Camp Mpal. Futbol Parc Catalana
Pl. de l'Angel
C. de l'Argenteria
Sta. Mª del Mar
Pl. Fossar de les Moreres
Av. Marquès de l'Argentera
C. d'Ocata
C. Duana
Parc de la Barceloneta
Pg. de la Barceloneta
Jaume I
Pl. d'Emili Vilanova
Pl. de Jacint Reventós
C. de la Maria
Pl. Santa Maria
Pla de Palau
C. dels Pinzon
C. Mediterrania
C. de Ginebra
Pl. de la Maquinista
Pg. de Salvat Papasseit
Pl. St.Just
C. de Lledó
Barceloneta
Pl. del Llagut
Pl. de Pompeu Gener
Pl. d'Antoni Genescà i Coromines
C. de la Ciutat
C. del Consolat del Mar
C. d'Isabel II
C. de Llauder
C. C. Reina Cristina
Pl. de Pau Vila
C. de la Maquinista
C. d'Andrea Doria
St. Miquel
Regomir
C. del Regomir
Pl. Traginers
Palau de Mar
Pg. de Joan de Borbó Comte de Barcelona
Pl. de la Font
C. de Sta. Lluïsa de Marillac
Pl. Veronica
Pl. d'Antonio López
Moll del Dipòsit
C. de Bàluard
C. d'Andrea Doria
Pl. d'Hilari Salvadó
C. de Palau
C. d'Ataülf
C. Marquet
C. Plata
Marina de Port Vell
Pl. la Barceloneta
C. de l'Atlàntida
C. de Josep Anselm Clavé
Pg. de Colom
C. d'en Gignàs
C. d'Avinyó
C. d'en Carabassa
C. Ample
C. de la Merce
Moll d'Espanya
Moll de la Barceloneta
C. de St. Carles
Pl. Poeta Bosca
C. de l'Almirall Cervera
C. Rull
C. dels Còdols
Pl. de la Mercè
Ronda del Litoral
de la Fusta
Pl. de l'Ictinio
C. de l'Almirall Aixada
C. Nou de St. Francesc
Pl. del Duc de Medinaceli
Moll de Bosch i Alsina
Dàrsena Nacional
Pg. d'Itaca
Dàrsena del Comerç
C. de l'Almirall Aixada
C. del Comte de Sta. Clara
Taradell
Estatua de Colón
Plaça Odissea
Moll del Rellotge
C. del Comte del Judici
anes
Maremàgnum
Rambla de Mar
C. Escar
C. Drassana
Platja de Sant Sebastià
del Mar
Port Vell
Pl. Palmeres
Moll de Barcelona
Moll de Marina
Platja de Sant Miquel
Moll de Barcelona
World Trade Center
Dàrsena de la Indústria
BC MAPS
www.bc-maps.com
info@bc-maps.com
Moll de Catalunya
Dàrsena de Sant Bertran
Moll Occidental
Dic Sec
Dic Flotant
Moll Oriental
Hotel W

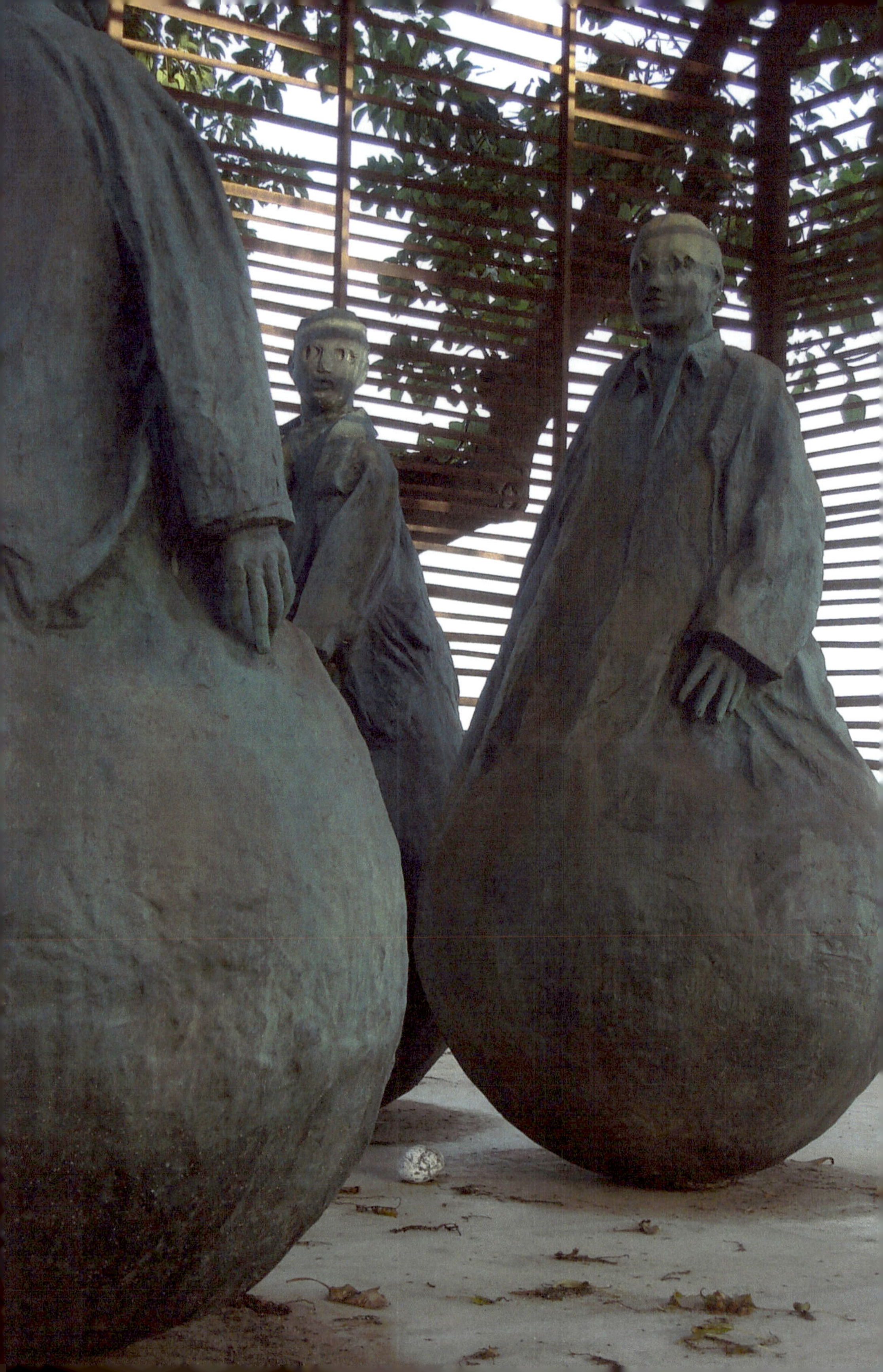

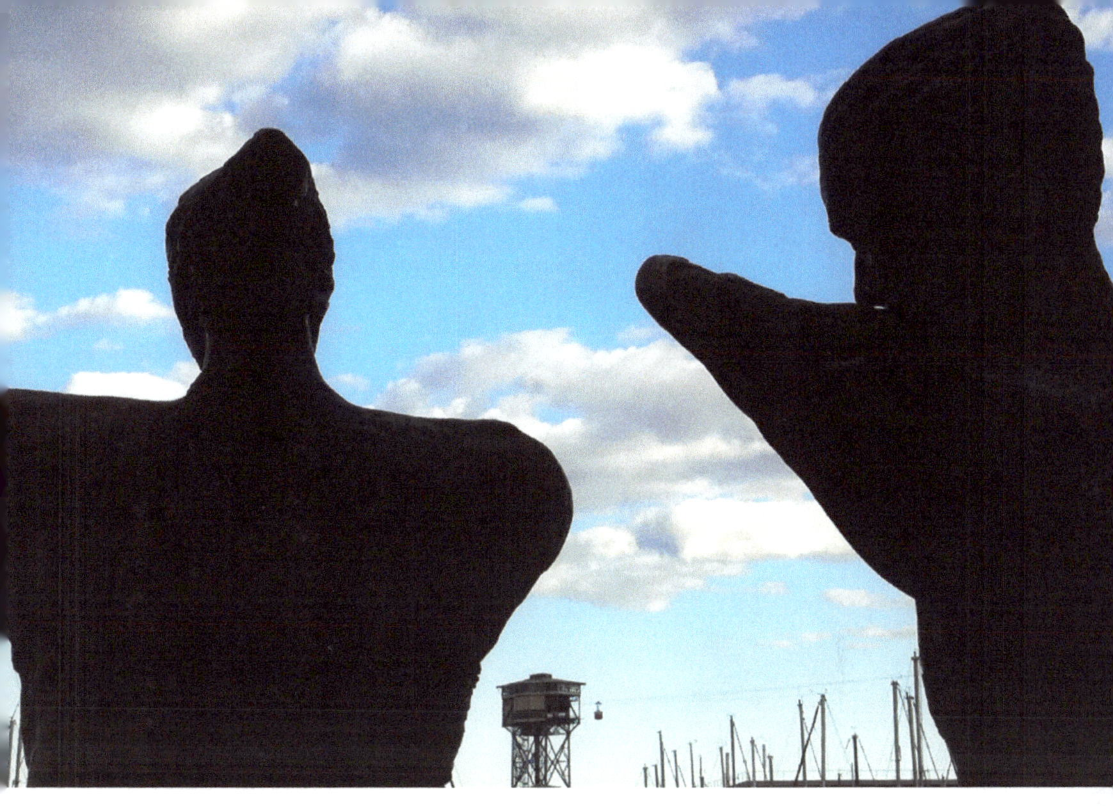

Why free art in Barcelona?

Art speaks to you. Good art inspires. Every civilisation has produced its own and though you don't need a doctorate to appreciate it, a little knowledge provides insight. Whether it argues for justice, entertains, educates or even serves as propaganda, art invites you to step beyond what you know and can experience with your senses, exploring that uncharted territory of the imagination that science has not yet mapped.

Being so valuable, it is often locked away, though this is incompatible with its purpose, which is to reach out, communicate and inspire, even ignite a spiritual response. And while free art is a great idea, not all great art is free.

The idea for these guides sprang from hard times. Whether in boom or recession, art remains fundamental. So should it be free? I think so, and that's why Barcelona Free Art takes you places where there is no admission fee.

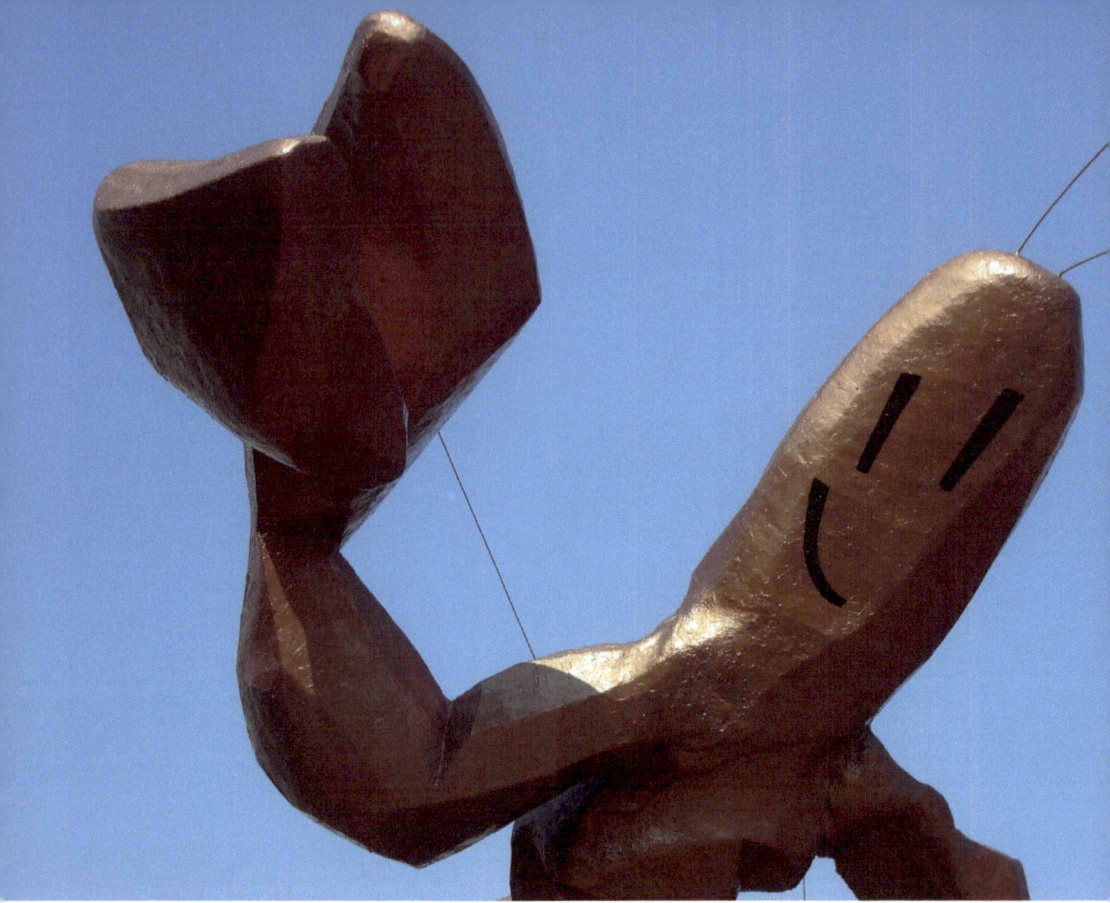

These guides offer history and information on the artists and their art to help you enjoy Barcelona all the more. There isn't much on Gaudí, Miró or Picasso—not that I don't like them, but I prefer to focus on art that is less talked about. While all the art in this book is free, sometimes spending a few euros will get you a better view.

The guides are designed to be followed on foot or by bike. If you have to take the metro occasionally, then buy a T1 ten-journey ticket, which at the time of publication costs under ten euros. There is no strict itinerary though the pieces are organised in a loose order for ease of walking.

All text and photos are original. When I reference something from somewhere else, I say so. Feel free to leave feedback and comments on the Barcelona Free Art blog (www.barcelonafreeart.net). If you'd like to sign up to our mailing list, go to Poble Sec Books (www.poblesecbooks.com).

Above all, enjoy Barcelona Free Art!

                         Kevin Booth

1. Columbus, a starting point

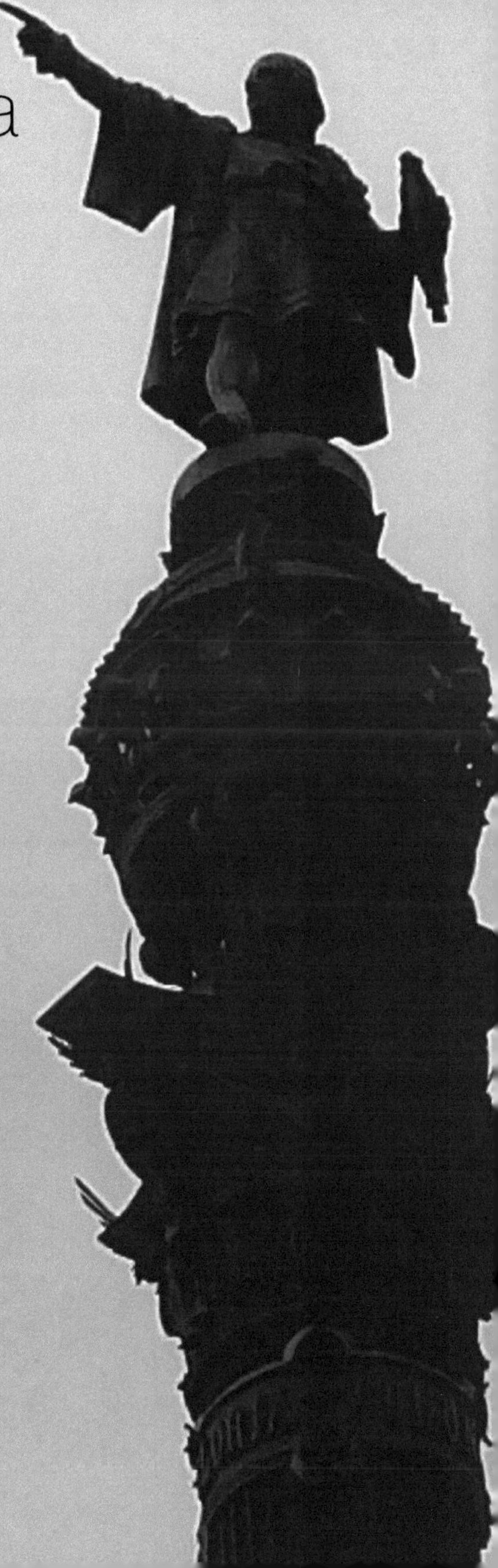

Columbus's column makes a good starting point as it's easy to find. It was here in Barcelona that he reported back to the Catholic Monarchs after discovering the new world. Once unveiled, this *Monument to Columbus*—designed by Gaietà Buïgas i Monravà and completed for the Barcelona World's Fair in 1888—became a city icon. A lift takes you up to the globe under the explorer's feet, from where you get a good view of the port and up the Ramblas.

The fifteen sculptors who created the column's fifty or so sculptural elements—representing Spain's three kingdoms (Aragon, Leon and Castile), the Principality of Catalonia, influential figures and scenes from Columbus's life, caravels, griffins, lions and the crowning seven-metre statue of Columbus himself by Rafael Atché —include important Catalan artists such as the Modernista sculptor, Josep Llimona i Bruguera. His medallion of explorer Vicente Yáñez Pinzón was undertaken after his return from studying in Rome. He would later create the moving piece *Desconsol* (*Grief*, 1907) that dominates the lake in front of the Catalan Parliament in the Parc de la Ciutadella. More of his work can be seen in Plaça Catalunya.

Cross the road in the direction of the harbour. The big wooden bridge you see ahead is called Rambla del Mar. On the other side is the Maremagnum entertainment centre, but we won't cross the bridge. Our first stop is to the right, out over the water.

Monument a Colom / Monument to Columbus (1888) designed by Gaietà Buïgas i Monravà, artworks created by Rafael Atché and numerous other artists. Bronze and stone. Plaza Portal de la Pau, s/n.

Coordinates: *41.375900, 2.177800*

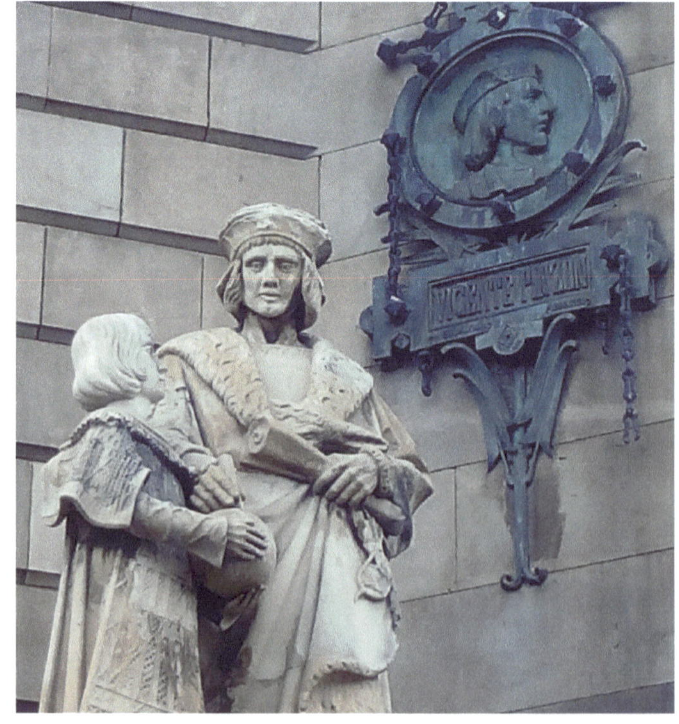

Josep Llimona i Bruguera's medallion of explorer Vicente Yáñez Pinzón was probably crafted as a young apprentice. His moving piece *Desconsol* (*Grief*, 1907) dominates the lake in front of the Catalan Parliament in the Parc de la Ciutadella.

Kevin Booth

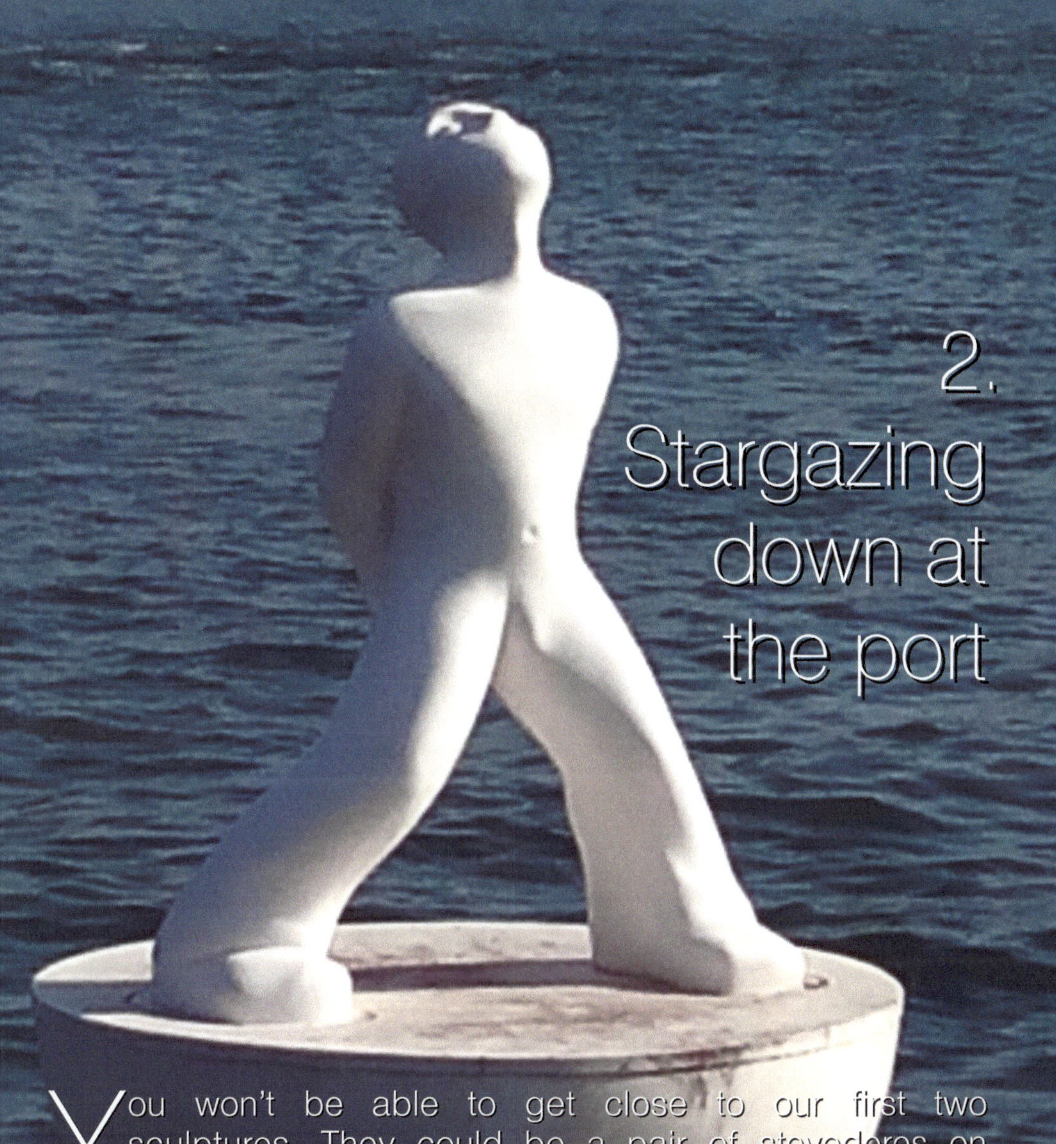

You won't be able to get close to our first two sculptures. They could be a pair of stevedores on deck, each marooned on a tiny pontoon. But they seem content to stand alone, legs astride, gazing up at the heavens. Placed too far out in the harbour to see many details, one thing that is only visible from the water is that each figure hides a coloured star behind its back. These apparently represent the different cultures that make up Barcelona. The artist has played with this figure in an iconic way over time, reproducing it in different materials and diverse settings. These figures are made of polyester and fibreglass.

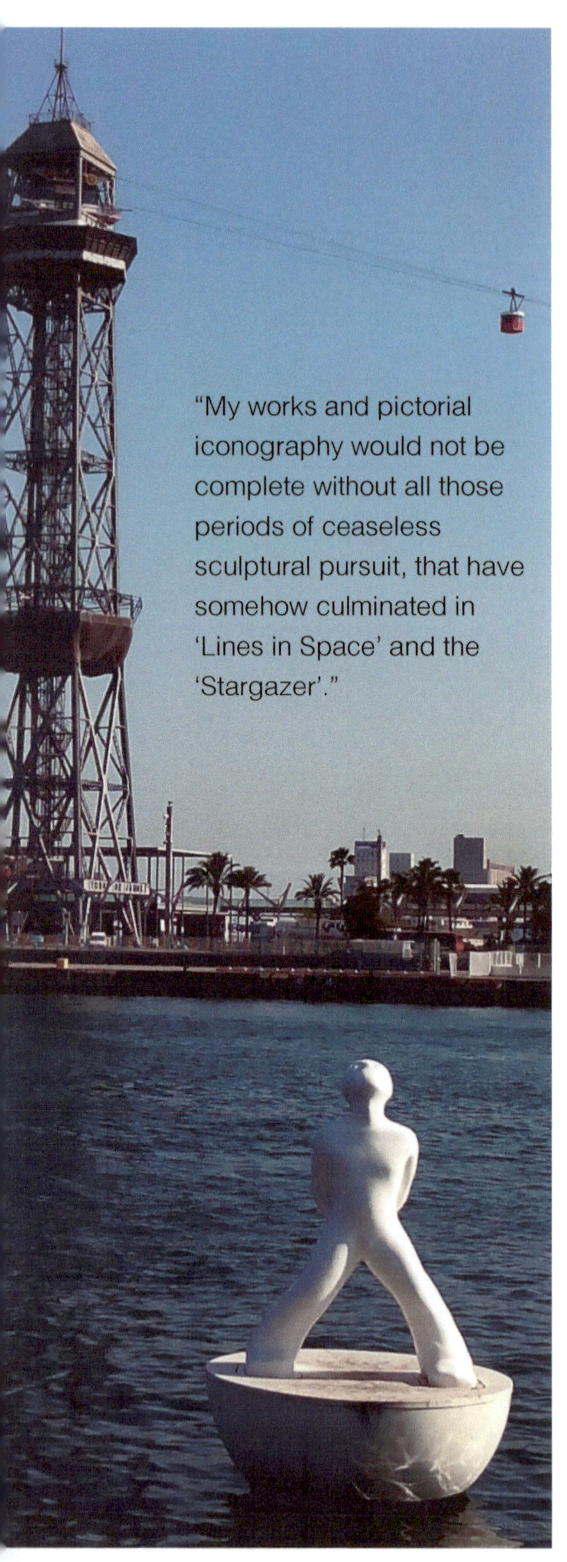

The artist, Robert Llimós, is a prolific Barcelona painter and sculptor. He was the son of an Impressionist painter, and figurative painting and drawing became his first passion. As an artist of the Spanish school known as New Figuration, he explains how, during the Spanish dictatorship, 'figuration' was a way of eluding the censor:

As if the history of art was a pendulum, my generation returned to the figurative elements in their works as we had things to say and social demands to make. It was a good way to bypass censorship while stating a message contrary to the regime, through recognisable elements opposing the prevailing informality of the fake left wing. This generation is the one that corresponds to German Expressionism, English pop and Italian transavantgarde, which we call New Figuration in Spain.

After experimenting with abstract and conceptual phases, the figurative is the form to

Kevin Booth

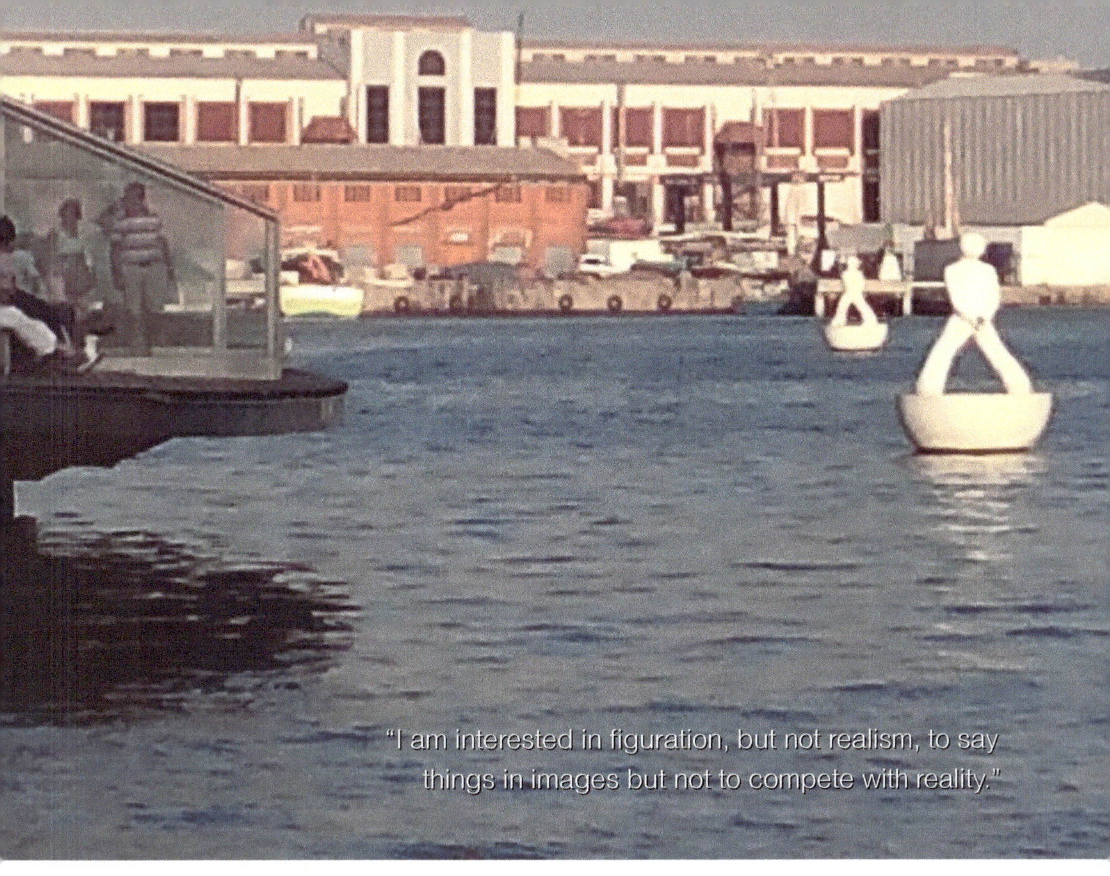

which he regularly returns, even as he rejects realism or the strongly representational. He sees his sculptural work as reaching a natural culmination in both the "Stargazer" pieces and his "Lines in Space", a series expressed sculpturally through *Marc* (*Frame*), installed nearby for the '92 Olympics. *Marc* has its twin, *Threshold*, which was installed in Atlanta, the city that hosted the Games four years after Barcelona, in 1996.

Llimós's most recent work was inspired by an apparent encounter with extraterrestrials, in Fortaleza, Brazil, in 2009. In fact, he sees this event as a response to the "Stargazers" series:

"[This work] is protecting the sea and requesting help from the sky. I have always thought that it would serve to make contact with the hereafter and that's how it has finally happened."

Miraestels / Stargazers (2006) by Robert Llimós. Polyester resin. Rambla de Mar, offshore.

Coordinates: *41.375026, 2.180467 / 41.374204, 2.182034*

References:
http://www.robertllimos.es

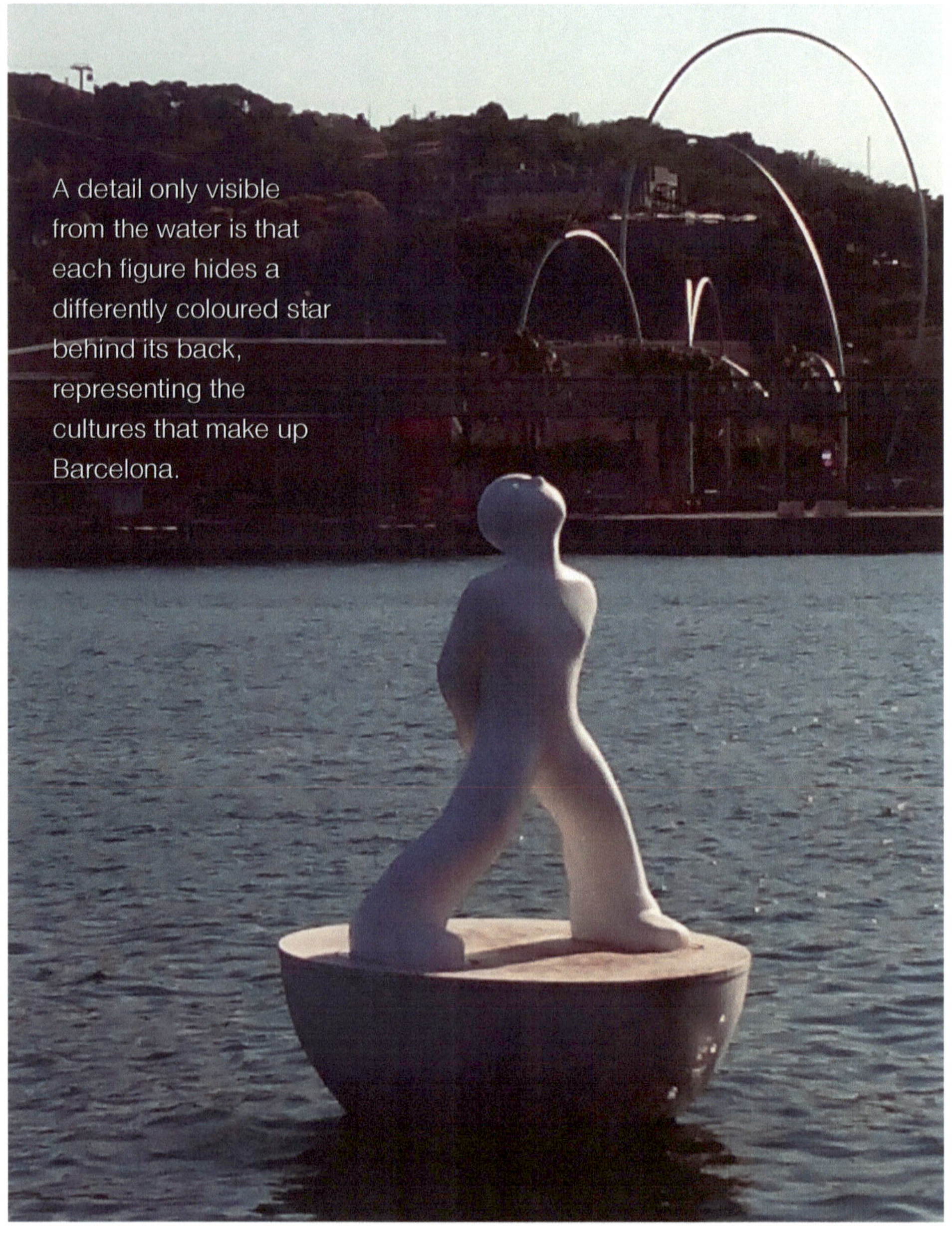

Kevin Booth

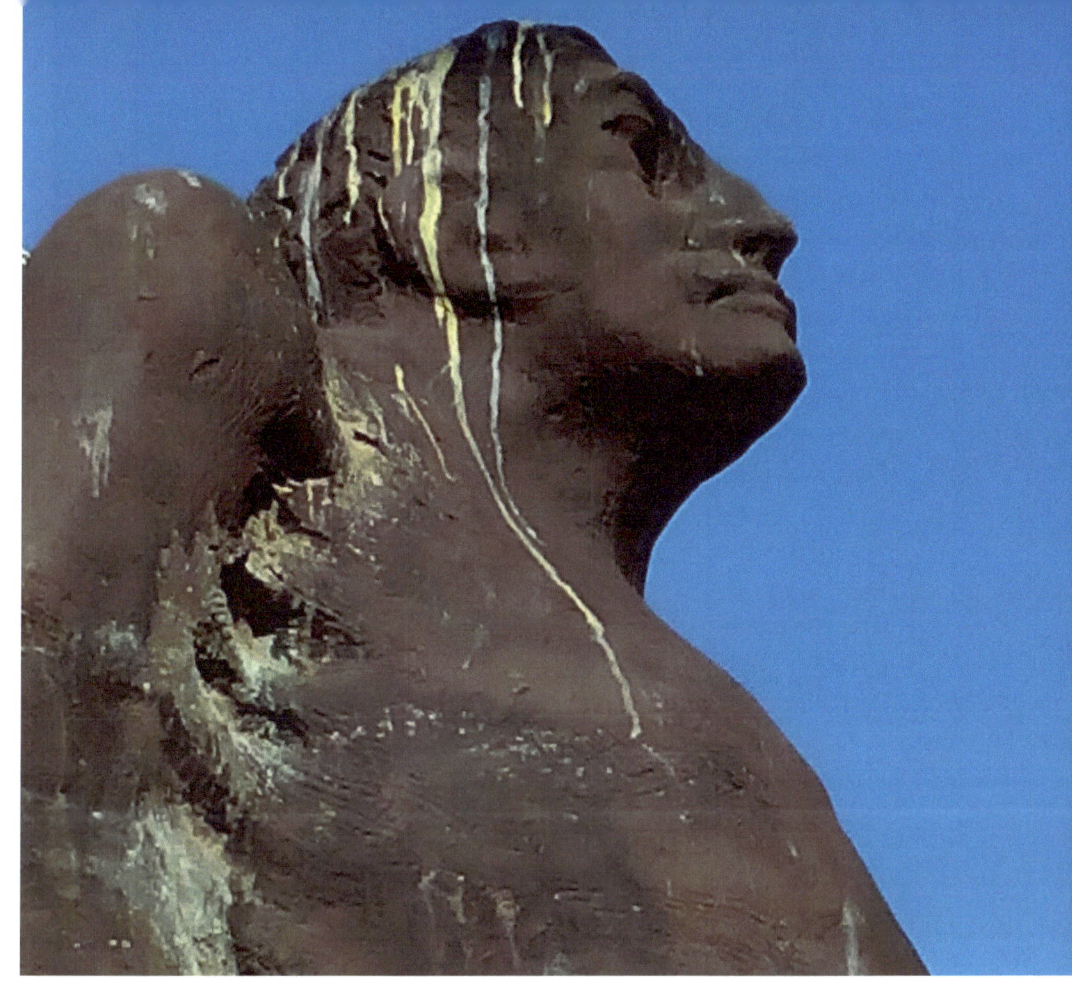

3. Anarchy on a classical plinth

From his internment in a naval orphanage after his father's death in a ship's stoking room, the sea cast a huge influence on Salvat-Papasseit's life.

Like a lone night watchman—as he was in his youth—the statue of Joan Salvat-Papasseit (1894–1924), one of Catalonia's preeminent poets, stands alone on the Moll de la Fusta (the timber wharf).

In 1909, the outbreak of the July rebellion—an anticlerical and anti-establishment uprising, christened the

Setmana tràgica or tragic week by the upper classes—gave the fifteen-year-old poet his formative political education. This conflict was sparked, among other smouldering issues, by an imbalance between Barcelona's moneyed and working classes as regards the mobilisation of reservists to fight in the Melilla War—Spain's belated attempt to relaunch an imperialist agenda after the loss of its colonies in Cuba and the Philippines. Apart from the fact that conscripts were mainly recruited from among the Catalans, wealthy young men could also buy their freedom from conscription for the staggering sum of six thousand *rals*, while among the poor, who earned less than twenty *rals* a day, many men with dependent families and no other means of subsistence were summoned to fight. The war's cause was also perceived by the people as being to protect mines owned by the loathed Marquis de Comillas and the Count Güell (no, the name is not coincidental). They both owned large factory-colonies within Catalonia, and enforced working conditions which, though Draconian, were fairly typical of nineteenth-century industrialism worldwide.

The clergy were seen as being hand-in-glove with the political and wealthier classes, and

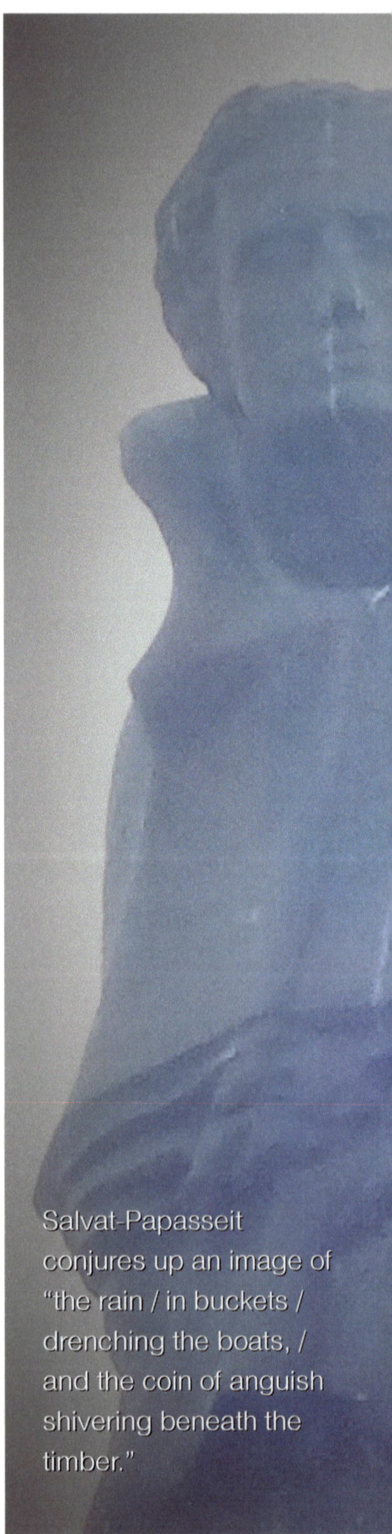

Salvat-Papasseit conjures up an image of "the rain / in buckets / drenching the boats, / and the coin of anguish shivering beneath the timber."

                    Kevin Booth

maintained a near-total ideological stranglehold on education, frustrating a new generation of collectivised and knowledge-thirsty workers. So the ensuing outbreak of violence was understandably directed against the Catholic Church. Yet even if plumes of smoke rose from many burning churches around Barcelona, casualties were limited to two deaths.

This was not the only tragedy to mark Salvat-Papasseit's early life: the death of his father, a ship's stoker, meant that, as a result of his mother's poverty, he was interned in a naval orphanage from the age of seven to twelve. There, he learned to read and write, and by the age of eighteen, he was penning unpaid articles from an anarchist slant under the *nom de plume* 'Gorkiano' (or 'Gorki-like') whilst earning his living as a night watchman down here on the timber dock.

In his poem "Nocturn per acordió" ("Nocturn for Accordion"), Salvat-Papasseit recalls seeing "the rain / in buckets / drenching the boats, / and the coin of anguish shivering beneath the timber; / beneath the flanders / and the pinewood, / beneath the sacred cedars".

Timber, right through the first half of the twentieth century, was a key commodity for both commerce and war. The timber section of the anarchist CNT union was the most powerful body of manpower in the city, even more so than the various army and police corps. This they proved on the outbreak of the fascist coup that led to the Spanish Civil War when, after "liberating" a large stash of arms, the CNT militia became a key force in defeating Francoist rebels throughout Catalonia.

Initially, when Barcelona was undergoing its hectic 1992 facelift, the City Council's plan was to install six sculptures in this newly rehabilitated waterside space. These were finally reduced to two, one at each end, which is fortuitous since Papasseit, on his basalt plinth, is of such a moody nature, he stands better alone.

The artist who created this sculpture, Robert Krier, is an exponent of New Classical architecture, a movement which sought to renovate historicist tendencies and return to more conservative values. This melds well with early-twentieth-century Noucentisme (the name coined in Italianate fashion after the century, the 1900s), which aimed to supersede Modernisme. The New Classical style sought to counteract the furious exuberances of turn-of-the-century

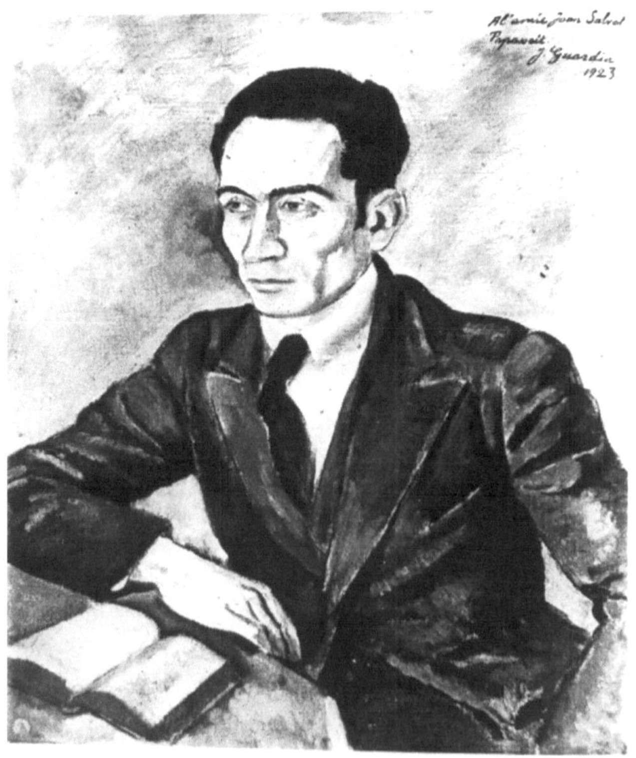

Portrait of Joan Salvat Papasseit a year before his death by the artist Jaume Guàrdia. 1923.

Kevin Booth

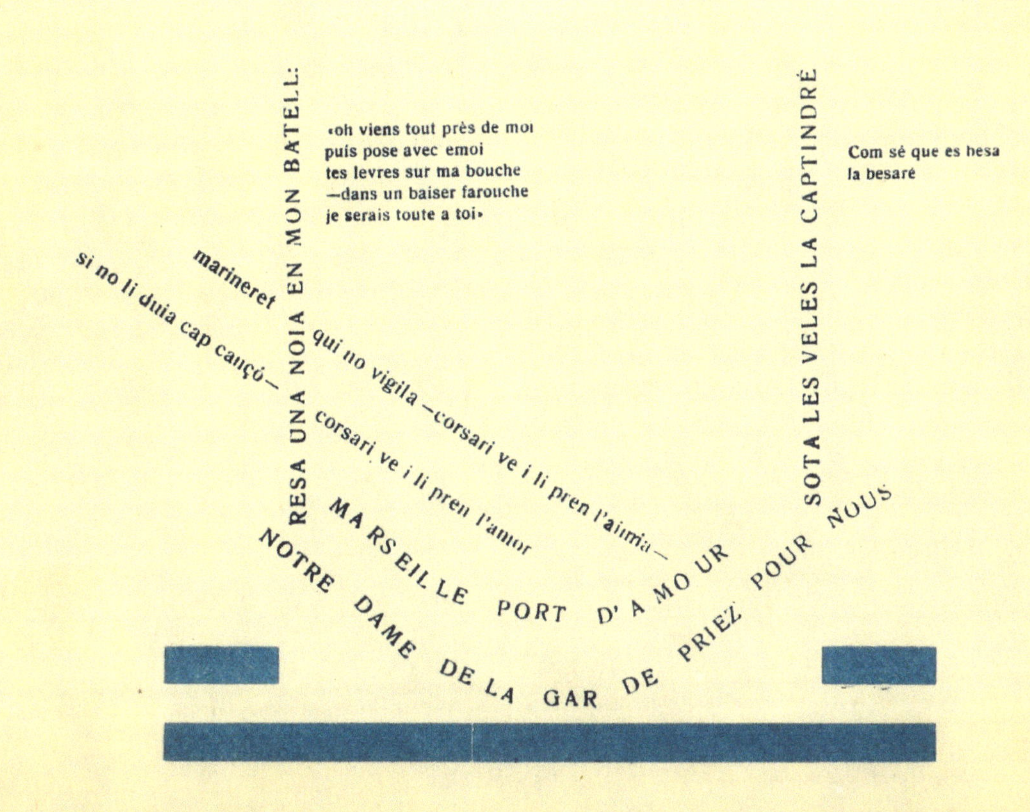

"Cal·ligrama 2", a type of visual poem where the text is arranged pictorially, from the book *El poema de la rosa als llavis* (*The Poem of the Rose on the Lips*, 1923) by Joan Salvat Papasseit.

expression—aesthetic explosions such as Gaudí's Sagrada Família at one end of the century, or Roy Lichenstein's pop-art *Barcelona's Head* at the other (and at the other end of this dock). The irony is that such a classicist sculptor should undertake a commission to depict a revolutionary anarchist poet.

The poem excerpt below, from "Nocturn per acordió" ("Nocturn for Accordion"), reveals Salvat-Papasseit reminiscing about his solitary nights on the timber dock.

NOCTURN PER ACORDIÓ:

[...]
Vosaltres no sabeu
què és
guardar fustes al moll.
Ni sabeu l'oració dels fanals dels vaixells
—que són de tots colors
com la mar sota el sol:
que no li calen veles.

NOCTURN FOR ACCORDION

[...]
You don't know
what it is
to watch the wood on the wharf.
Neither do you know the prayer of the ships' lights
—which are so many colours
like the sea beneath the sun:
which needs no sails.

You can find more translations of Salvat Papasseit's poetry at: *http://www.anglo-catalan.org/downloads/acsop-monographs/issue02.pdf.*

A Joan Salvat Papasseit / To Joan Salvat Papasseit (1992) by Robert Krier. Bronze. Moll de Bosch i Alsina (Moll de la fusta).

Coordinates: *41.376401, 2.179634*

References:

http://www.anglo-catalan.org/downloads/acsop-monographs/issue02.pdf

 Kevin Booth

4.
A much-loved couple

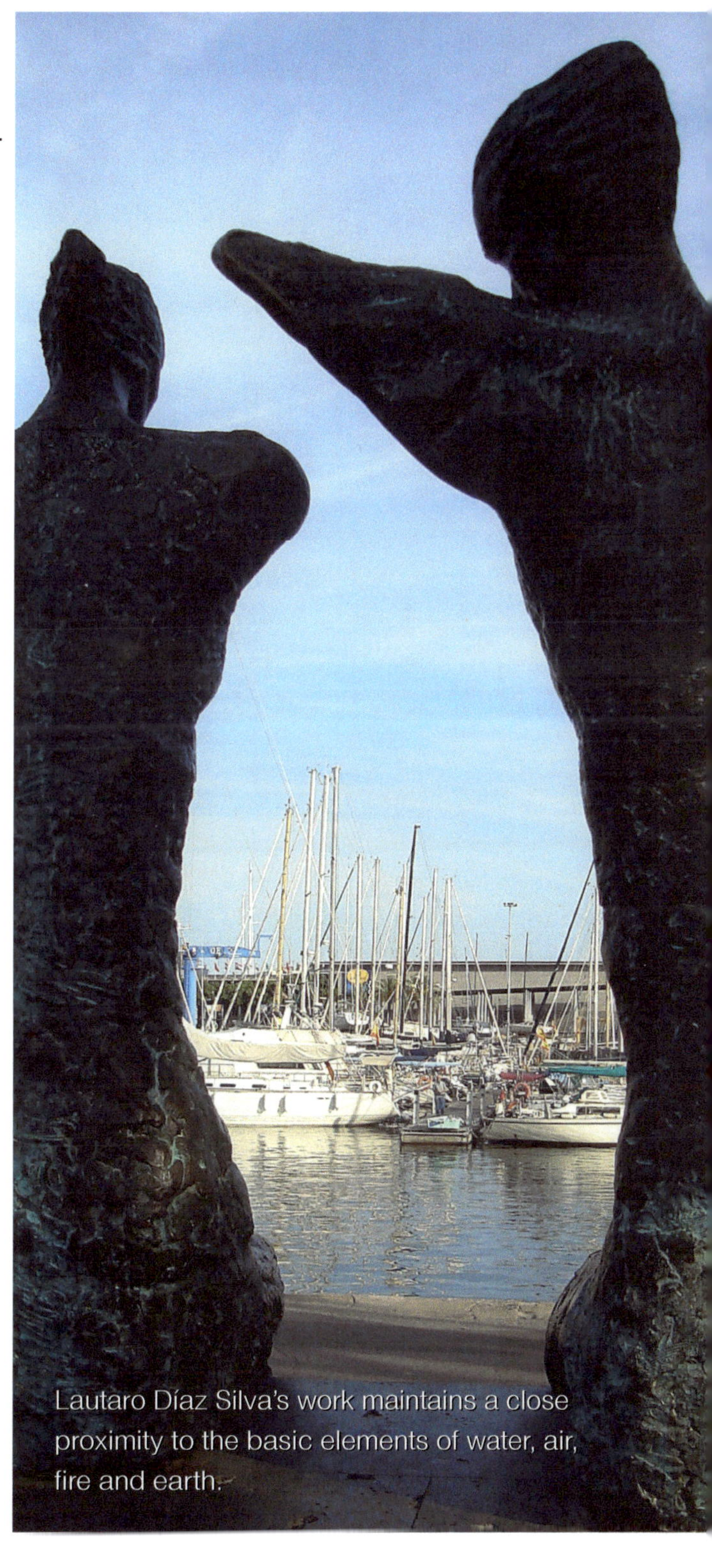

Lautaro Díaz Silva's work maintains a close proximity to the basic elements of water, air, fire and earth.

Strolling further along the Moll de la fusta (timber dock), you'll come across this congruent couple by Chilean artist Lautaro Díaz Silva, another photo favourite for those interested in the free sculpture which the Barcelona waterfront offers.

Subtly abstracted while conveying perfectly that intense intimacy born of long-standing trust, these figures in bronze, finished in a greenish patina, depict a couple, possibly lovers, observing the sea. An interesting detail is the man's

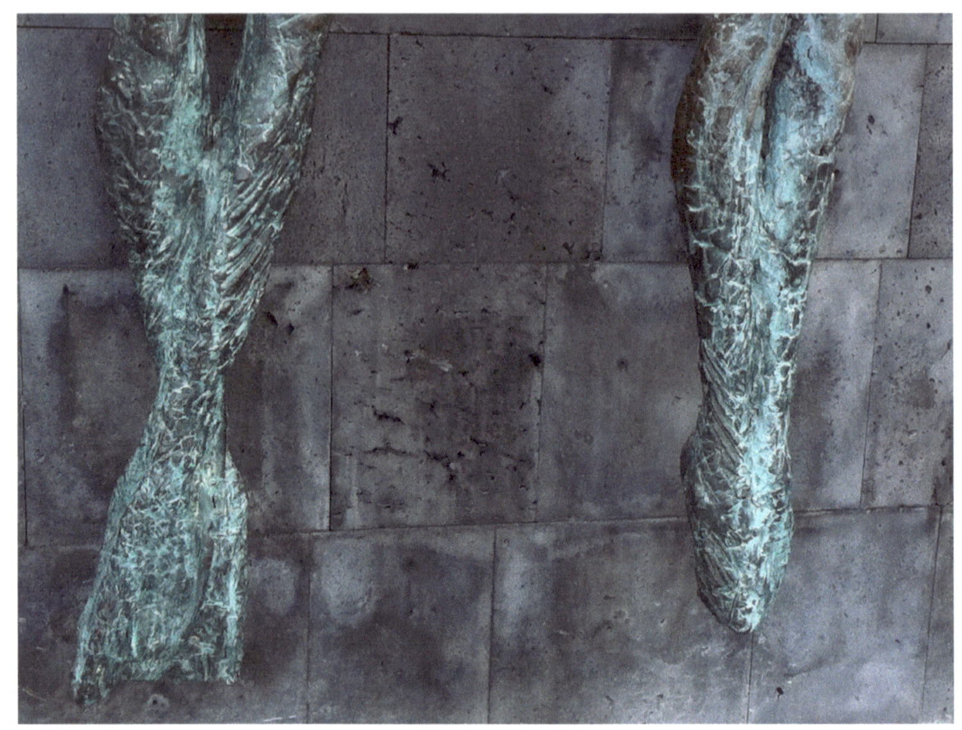

Note the detail of the man's feet, which resemble a fish's tail. Merman or expressionism?

feet, which almost resemble a fish's tail. Is he a merman who has swum up out of the waves to court his earthbound lover, or are they both mer-folk, who have come ashore to watch the sunrise together? Díaz's decision not to raise the pair onto a pedestal works well to bring them closer to their public.

The artist's passionate expressionism is equally as deft and sculptural in the way he applies paint to his very tactile canvases. His figurative work is similarly pensive. The motif of a male and female couple is recurrent, whether convulsive and passionate, or in repose. In his abstract works and videos, he makes vibrant use of colour and iconic forms that recur in an almost ritualistic manner while the basic elements of water, air, fire and earth are always in close proximity.

Kevin Booth

Now resident in Germany, Lautaro Díaz Silva focuses more on oils and video, exhibiting regularly in Berlin and Barcelona among other cities. Other Barcelona works include a *Homage to Salvador Allende*, installed in Plaça Salvador Allende, on 11 September 1997—to mark the twenty-fifth anniversary of the *coup d'état* that replaced Allende's government with Pinochet's bloody dictatorship. You can see an identical version of it—Allende's head mounted on the wall—in the Camp de Mart, in Tarragona. Another installation, *To Victor Jara*, is located in Barcelona's Plaça Karl Marx.

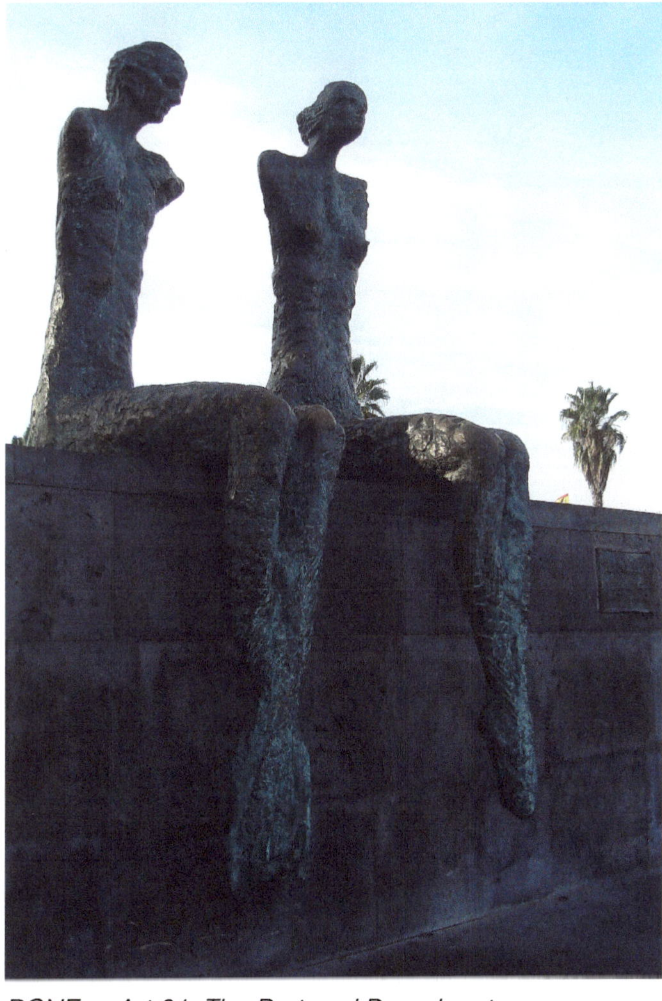

Vaguely reminiscent of Giacometti's spindly forms, Lautaro Diaz's figures convey an intimacy in their spatial relationships.

La Parella / The Couple (1998) by Lautaro Díaz Silva. Bronze. Moll de la Fusta.

Coordinates: *41.378442, 2.181313*

References:

   http://www.lautaro-diaz.de

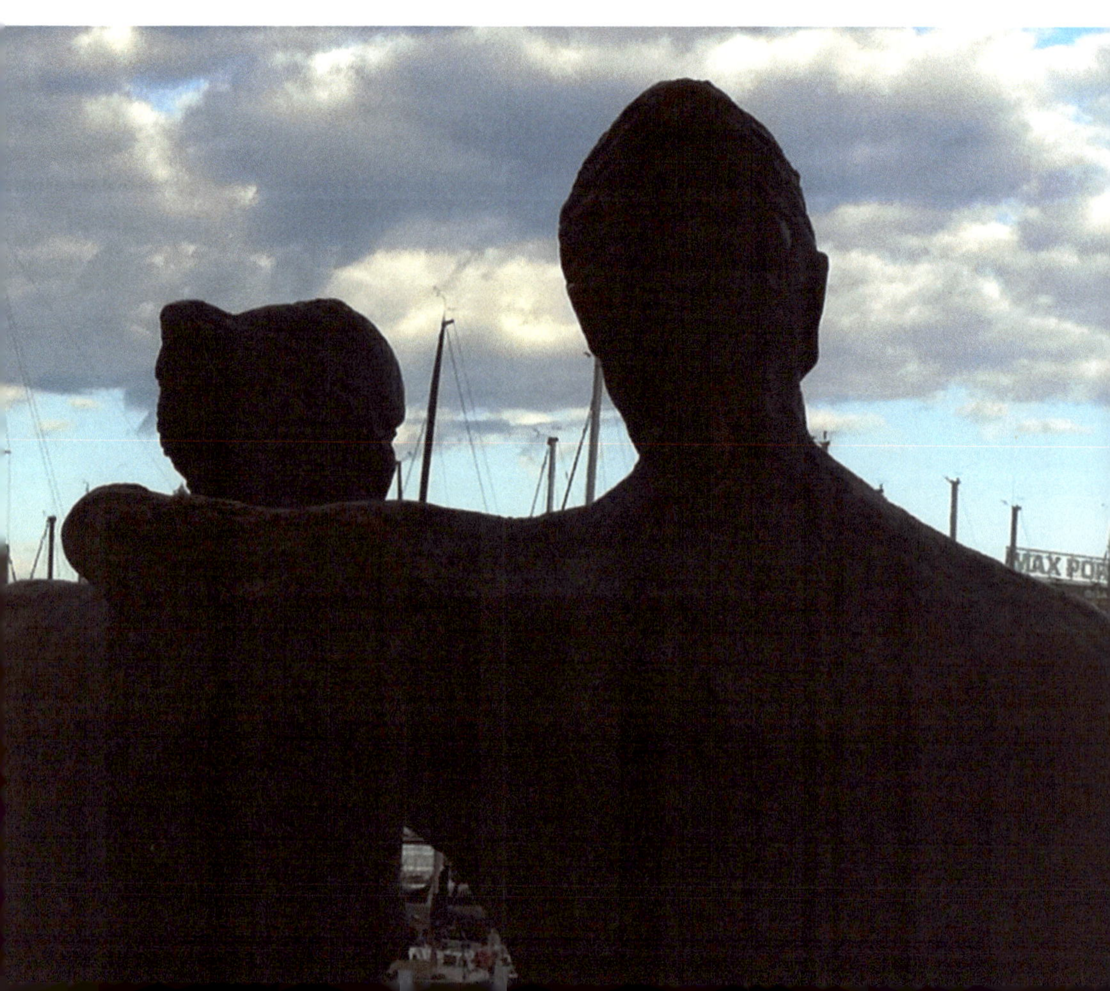

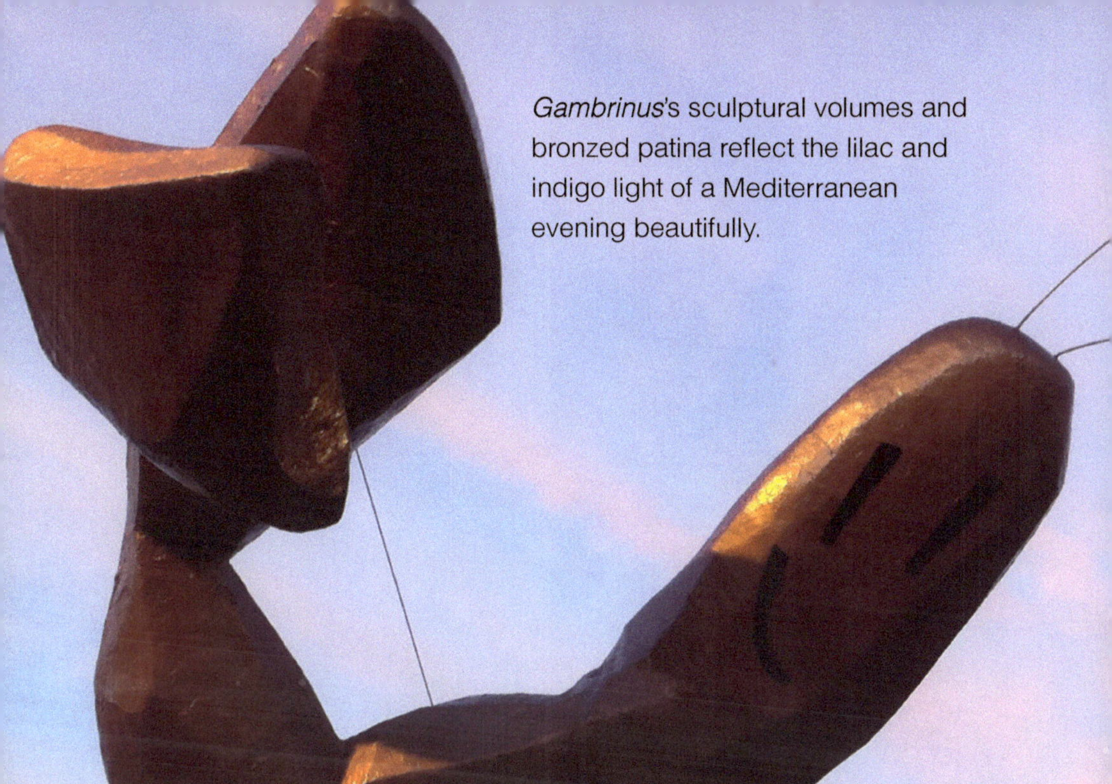

Gambrinus's sculptural volumes and bronzed patina reflect the lilac and indigo light of a Mediterranean evening beautifully.

5. Dancing prawn

Many's the town that cheerfully flaunts some huge and dreadful object on its loftiest hilltop. Normally made of concrete or fibreglass, the monstrosity strives to fulfil its illusory destiny as a cultural icon. So Goulburn, Australia, brims with pride over a fifteen-metre-high Merino sheep, an outsize barrel takes pride of place in Okinawa, Japan, while Flanders, New York, sports a giant cement duck. Whether or not they were despised for blighting the landscape at the time of installation, they generally end up being accepted by the locals, even occupying a warm fuzzy spot in the town's heart.

Of such species, I would argue that Barcelona's denizen is one of the least offensive you'll find—positively charming, in fact. The city's giant prawn (*La Gamba*: though

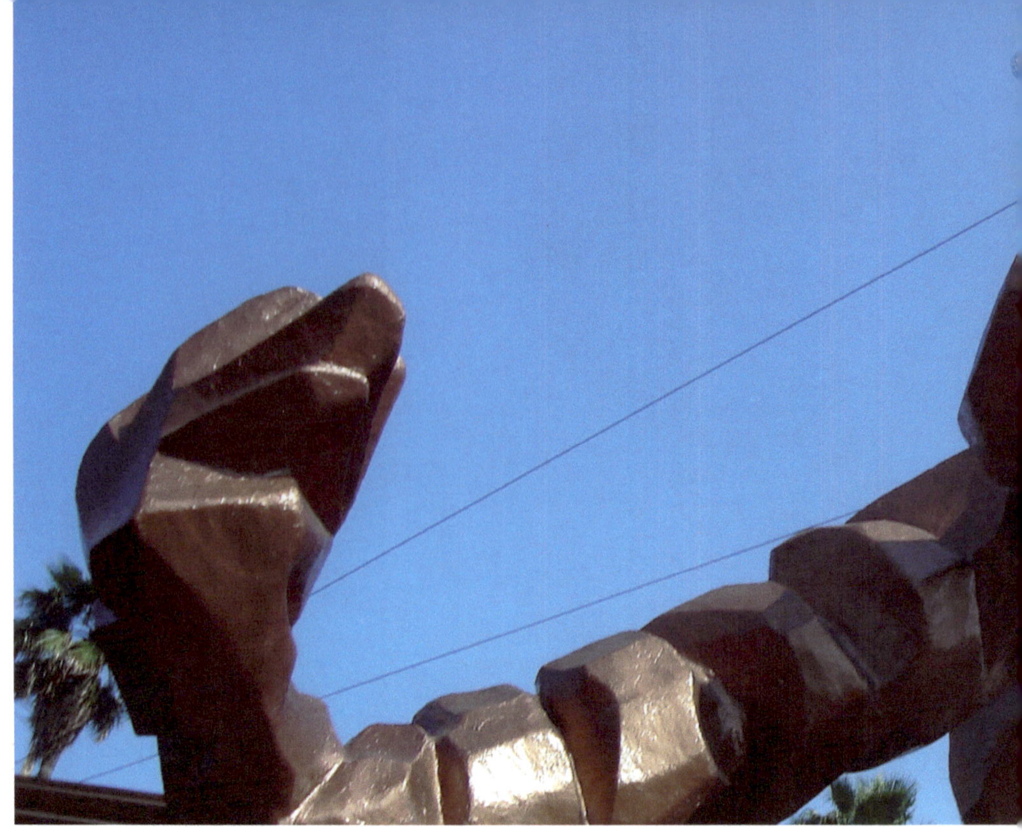

technically it doesn't count as a prawn—unless you're in Dublin Bay, when it does—but as an *escamarlà* or langoustine, which itself is not to be confused with the Spanish *langostino* as that is an entirely separate controversy) is affectionately known as "Gambrinus" after the restaurant it was designed to crown. It is by the Catalan designer and artist, Xavier Mariscal, and has a whimsically comical air that makes it the perfect seafront companion to Lichtenstein's cartoonish *Barcelona's Head* nearby.

Mariscal is the artist who arguably put Barcelona on the international design circuit (well, discounting a certain German who designed a chair) as the creator of its famous Olympic mascot, *Cobi.* So he surely deserves a decent position on Barcelona's *primera línea de mar* (seafront).

Though inaugurated in 1989, the restaurant Gambrinus barely outlived the end of the Olympic Games. Following this, the giant prawn was dragged wearily through the courts regarding the question of ownership, which was finally decided in favour of Barcelona City Council.

                    Kevin Booth

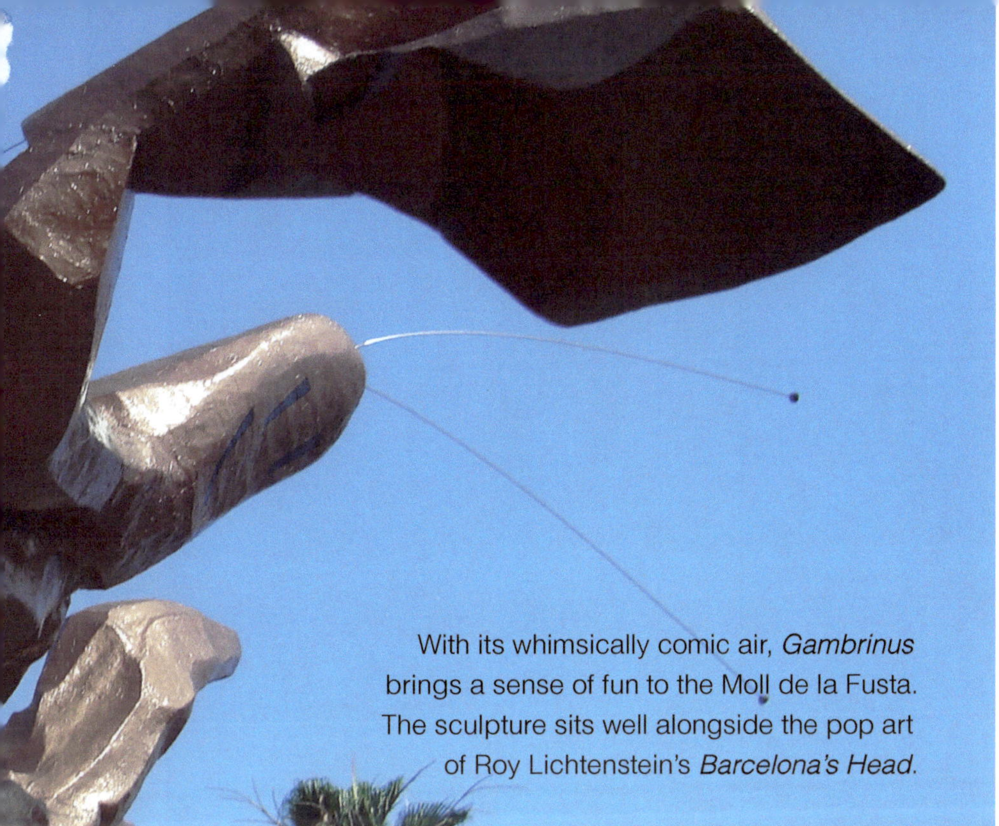

With its whimsically comic air, *Gambrinus* brings a sense of fun to the Moll de la Fusta. The sculpture sits well alongside the pop art of Roy Lichtenstein's *Barcelona's Head*.

Restored to its original site in 2004, *Gambrinus* (the name originally belongs to a northern-European folk figure who was falsely attributed with having invented beer) has now become a popular and fitting symbol for the city where seafood paella is a common staple.

The Vila Olímpica (Olympic Village) hosts other Mariscal sculptures, such as *Cobi*, the 1992 Olympic mascot, a Cubist-inspired depiction of a Catalan sheepdog, whose name is derived from the acronym for the Barcelona Olympic Organising Committee (COOB). For those who know where to look, this Olympic mascot also hides in the white *trencadís* (the broken-tile mosaic pioneered by Gaudí) of one of the chimneys on Palau Güell, in Carrer Nou de la Rambla. This building, built 1886–1890, was partially restored in 1992, the year of Barcelona's Olympic Games, when an anonymous restorer decided to encipher the year of restoration into her or his work.

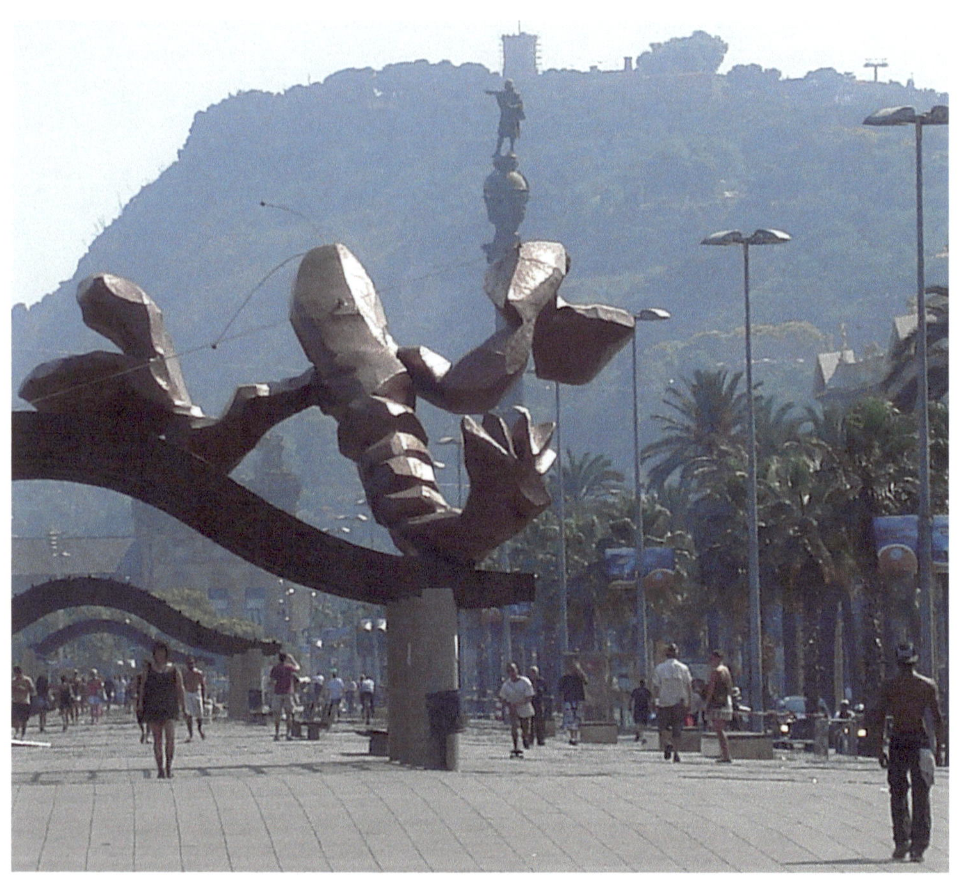

The series of restaurants along Moll de la Fusta,
for which Gambrinus was conceived, folded
shortly after the Olympic Games, and the
esplanade was remodelled.

La Gamba / Gambrinus (1989) by Xavier Mariscal. Steel
and fibreglass. Passeig de Colom, 7.
Coordinates: *41.380148, 2.181716*
Cobi, 1992. Parc del Port Olimpic, s/n.
Coordinates: *41.389276, 2.198678*
References:

http://www.mariscal.com
http://www.lavanguardia.com/local/barcelona/2015031
8/54428229882/cobi-gaudi.html

　　　　　　　　Kevin Booth

6. Lichtenstein on Modernisme: a comic take

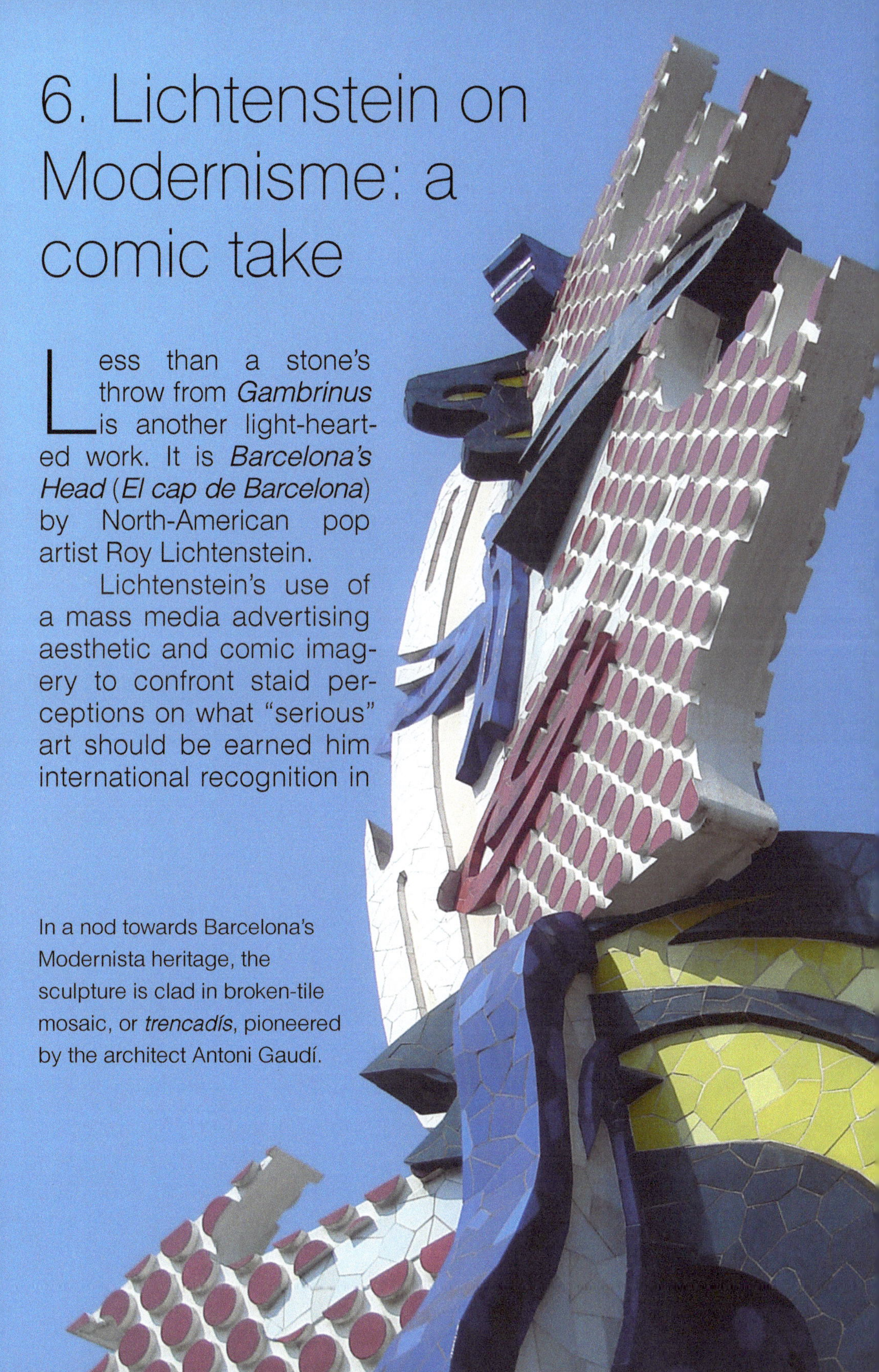

Less than a stone's throw from *Gambrinus* is another light-hearted work. It is *Barcelona's Head* (*El cap de Barcelona*) by North-American pop artist Roy Lichtenstein.

Lichtenstein's use of a mass media advertising aesthetic and comic imagery to confront staid perceptions on what "serious" art should be earned him international recognition in

In a nod towards Barcelona's Modernista heritage, the sculpture is clad in broken-tile mosaic, or *trencadís*, pioneered by the architect Antoni Gaudí.

the sixties. In Michael Kimmelman's words, the artist:

> *"seemed to critics like the equivalent of a giant pin aimed at the hot-air balloon of Abstract Expressionism, with its soul-searching claims and emphasis on the eloquence of a painter's touch".*

Barcelona's Head shows this same debt towards comic iconography yet is a far more complex development of this vocabulary. Still present are the bold lines, bright colours and dot background—recalling the Ben-Day process used in older comic-book printing—which characterise earlier satirical works such as *Whaam!* (1963) and *Drowning Girl* (1963). Yet the work also acknowledges Cubism and Modernisme, reflecting an engagement with the world of "serious" art.

The sculpture, a commission for the 1992 Summer Olympics, was physically constructed over two years by Diego Delgado Rajado, a Spanish artist from Badajoz. It is inspired by and pays homage to Catalan Modernisme—the local brand of Art Nouveau. This can be seen in its nod towards *trencadís*, or broken-tile mosaic, a Modernist technique pioneered by the architect Antoni Gaudí. Though many Art Nouveau architects used ceramic tiles as a way of transferring the bright and enduring

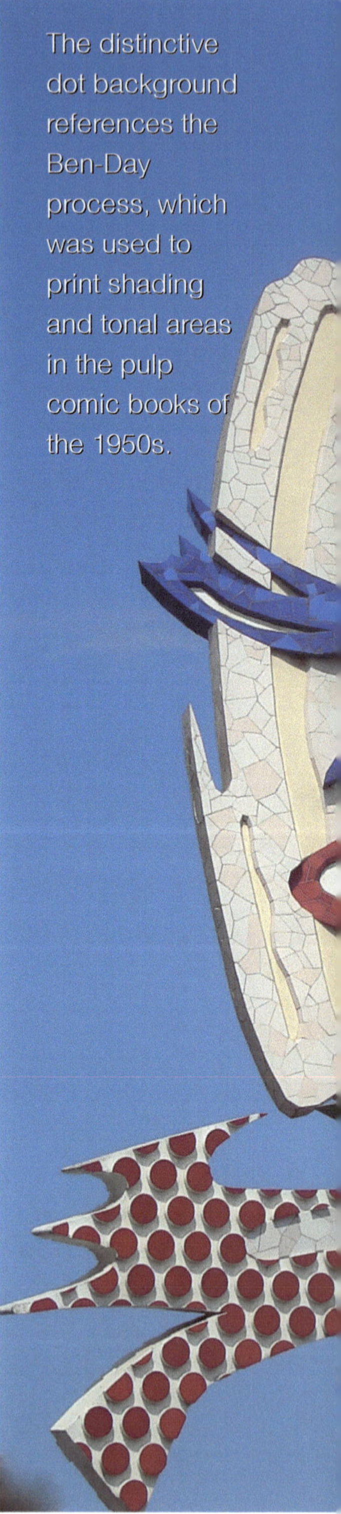

The distinctive dot background references the Ben-Day process, which was used to print shading and tonal areas in the pulp comic books of the 1950s.

        Kevin Booth

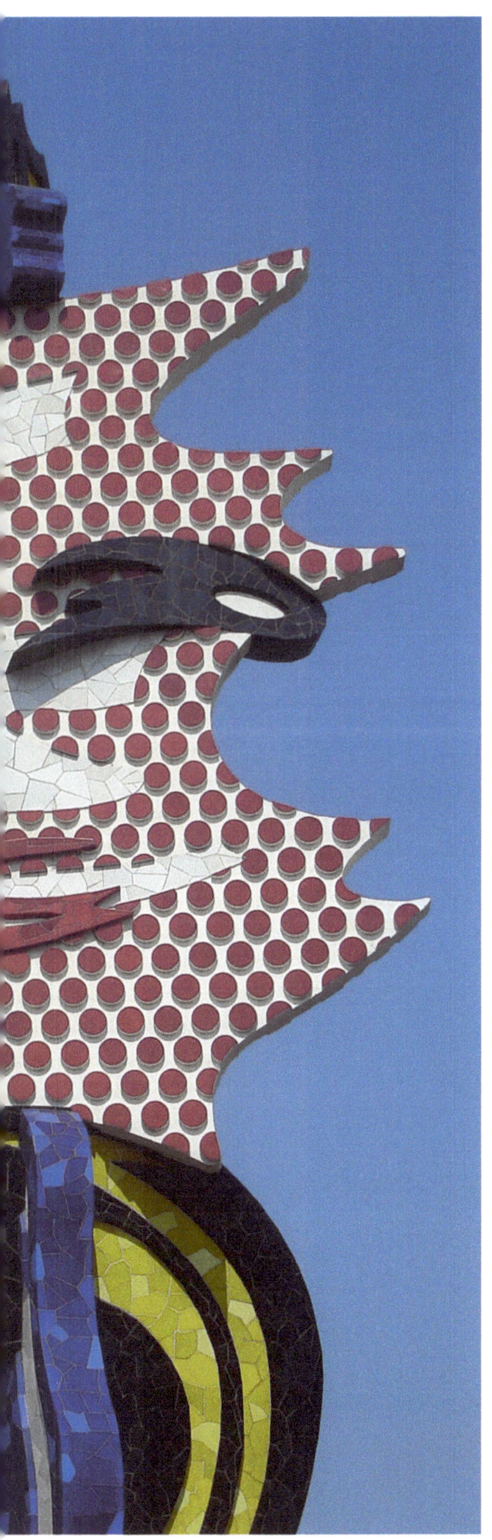

colours found in pottery glazes onto their buildings, Gaudí is credited with inventing *trencadís*. On visiting the mosaic workshop of Lluís Brú i Salelles, who was undertaking commissions for his buildings, Gaudí is supposed to have exclaimed: "In handfuls, you must apply [the ceramic shards]; other-wise, we'll never be done!"

Fifteen metres high by six wide, *Barcelona's Head* is made of eight large blocks of prefabricated artificial stone, stainless steel staples and ceramic cladding. It forms part of a series entitled "Brushstrokes", in which the works convey the impression of a brisk, free execution.

Other works from the "Brushstrokes" series can be found in US cities including Philadelphia, Boston, Portland, Columbus and Los Angeles, as well as internationally in Singapore, Tokyo, Paris and the Museo National Centro de Arte Reina Sofía, in Madrid.

El Cap de Barcelona / Barcelona's Head (1992) by Roy Lichtenstein and Diego Delgado Rajado. Artificial stone, steel and ceramic. Passeig de Colom, corner of Pas Sota Muralla, Port Vell.

Coordinates: *41.380914, 2.182454*

References:

http://www.lichtensteinfoundation. org
'Roy Lichtenstein at the Met', excerpted from Michael Kimmelman's "Portraits, Talking with Artists at the Met, The Modern, The Louvre and Elsewhere", from an interview given to the New York Times
(http://www.lichtensteinfoundation .org/kimmelman1.htm)

Made of eight blocks of prefabricated artificial stone, stainless steel staples and ceramic cladding, *Barcelona's Head* took Badajoz artist Diego Delgado Rajado two years to produce.

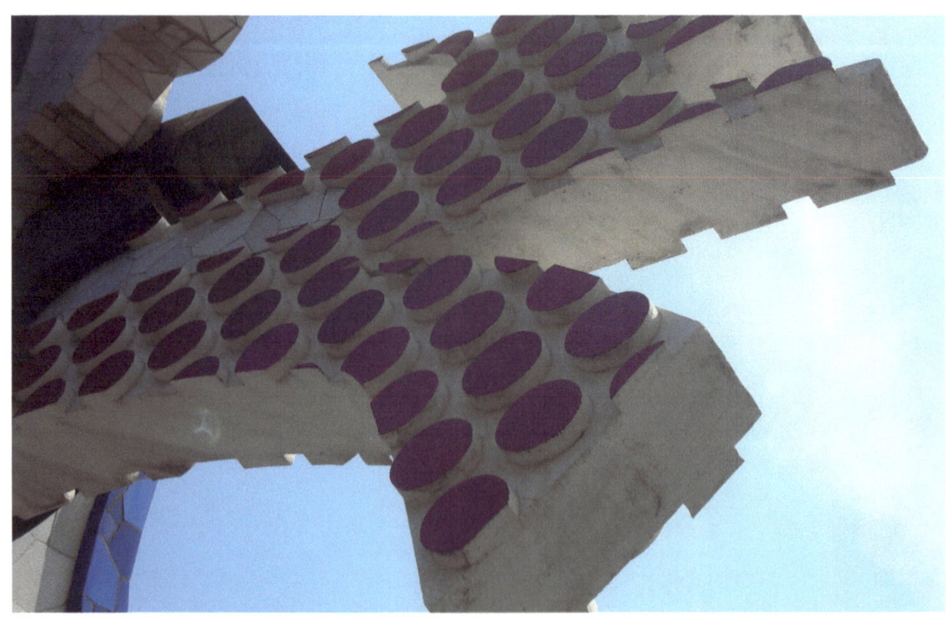

Kevin Booth

"Urban Configurations" and the Olympic legacy

Though the Olympics are the world's foremost sporting event, Barcelona 1992 did as much for the city's public art as for its sports facilities. Massive investments transformed the urban landscape almost beyond recognition. Nowhere was this more apparent than in the demolition of the Somorrostro neighbourhood and on Barceloneta shoreline. Yet out of this upheaval came exciting projects such as "Configuraciones urbanes" ("Urban Configurations"), a series of installations that aimed to form a chain between two historically linked Barcelona neighbourhoods—La Ribera and Barceloneta.

This historical association was forged in 1714, on the occasion of Catalonia's defeat in the War of the Spanish Succession. After his victory over the Catalan, British and other forces, Philip V of Spain ordered the neighbourhood of La Ribera be partially razed to make way for

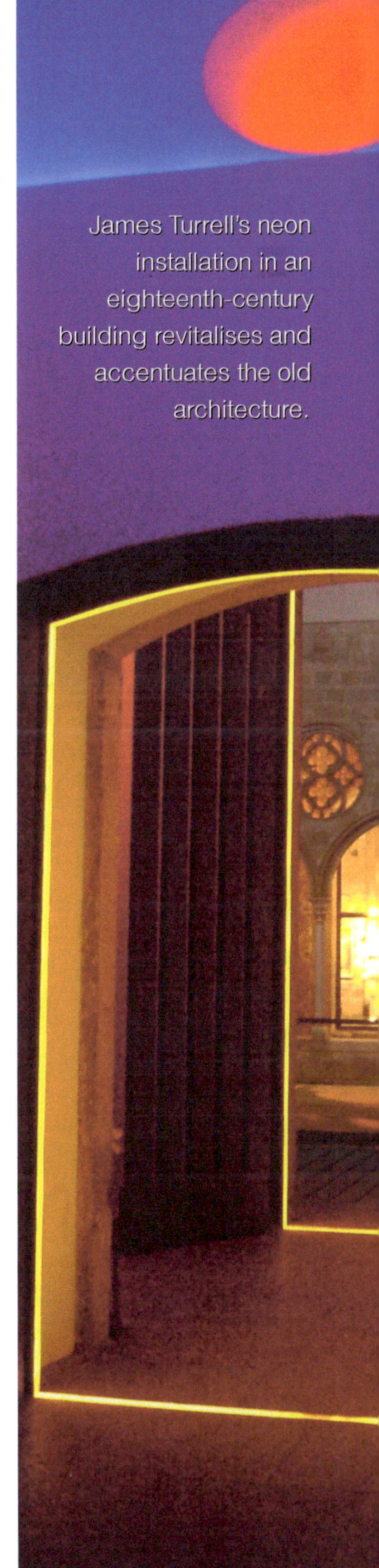

James Turrell's neon installation in an eighteenth-century building revitalises and accentuates the old architecture.

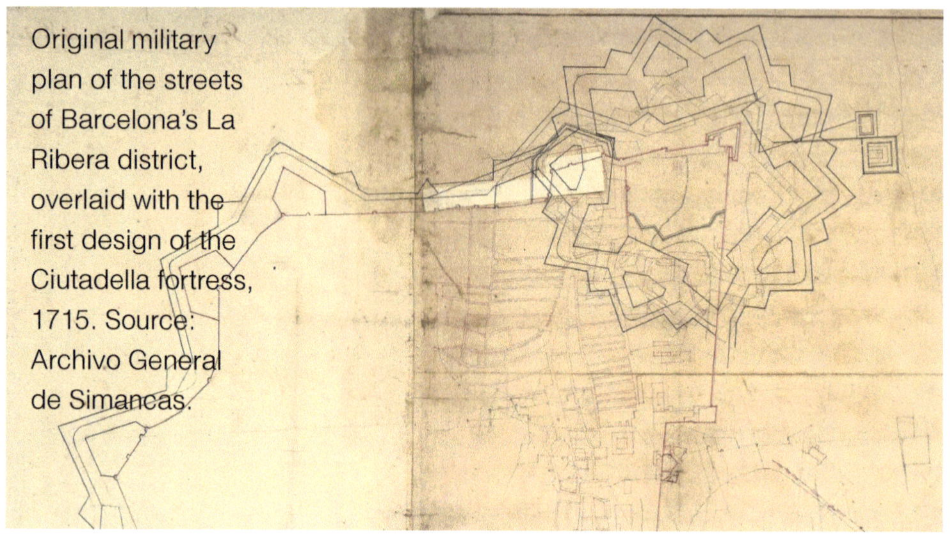

construction of the Ciutadella—a fortress designed (like the Montjuïc fortress) not so much to protect citizens from outside danger but to suppress further civil insurrection. It took a couple of years before the ousted former residents of La Ribera were assigned plots of land on the Barceloneta sand spit, where a fishing village had been haphazardly growing since the Renaissance. Over the ensuing years, a shanty town developed. Then, in 1753, a rational new street plan was implemented based on the plans of Joris Prosper van Verboom—the Flemish military engineer who was primarily responsible for Barcelona's fall in 1714. Housing priority was given to residents engaged in activities connected to the sea.

Over two hundred years later, in the lead-up to the 1992 Barcelona Summer Olympics, the Somorrostro neighbourhood and the Poble Nou and Barceloneta seafront were redesigned to open up the shoreline to the city and remodel Barcelona's neglected port and beaches.

"Urban Configurations", a permanent open-air collection of eight works, conceived by Barcelona curator Gloria Moure, was inaugurated just days before the Olympics. This show sought to combine foreign, Spanish and Catalan artists while bequeathing works to the city that would epitomise creative tension, art that was accessible to its

                    Kevin Booth

public, in harmony with its physical and human environment and engaged in a dialogue with the space in which it was installed. The results are one indoor and seven outdoor sculptural installations, by one Catalan, one Spanish and six international artists.

Heading from Carrer Comerç down towards the beach, these works are:

i. *Deuce Coop* by James Turrell. This US artist's neon installation in an eighteenth-century building—now a community centre—revitalises and accentuates the old architecture. It contains an iconic Turell reference in the oculus and use of light. Its lustrous tranquillity encourages the viewer to take ample time to appreciate the installation fully at a meditative pace. Installed in the community centre, the installation is only available during opening times and

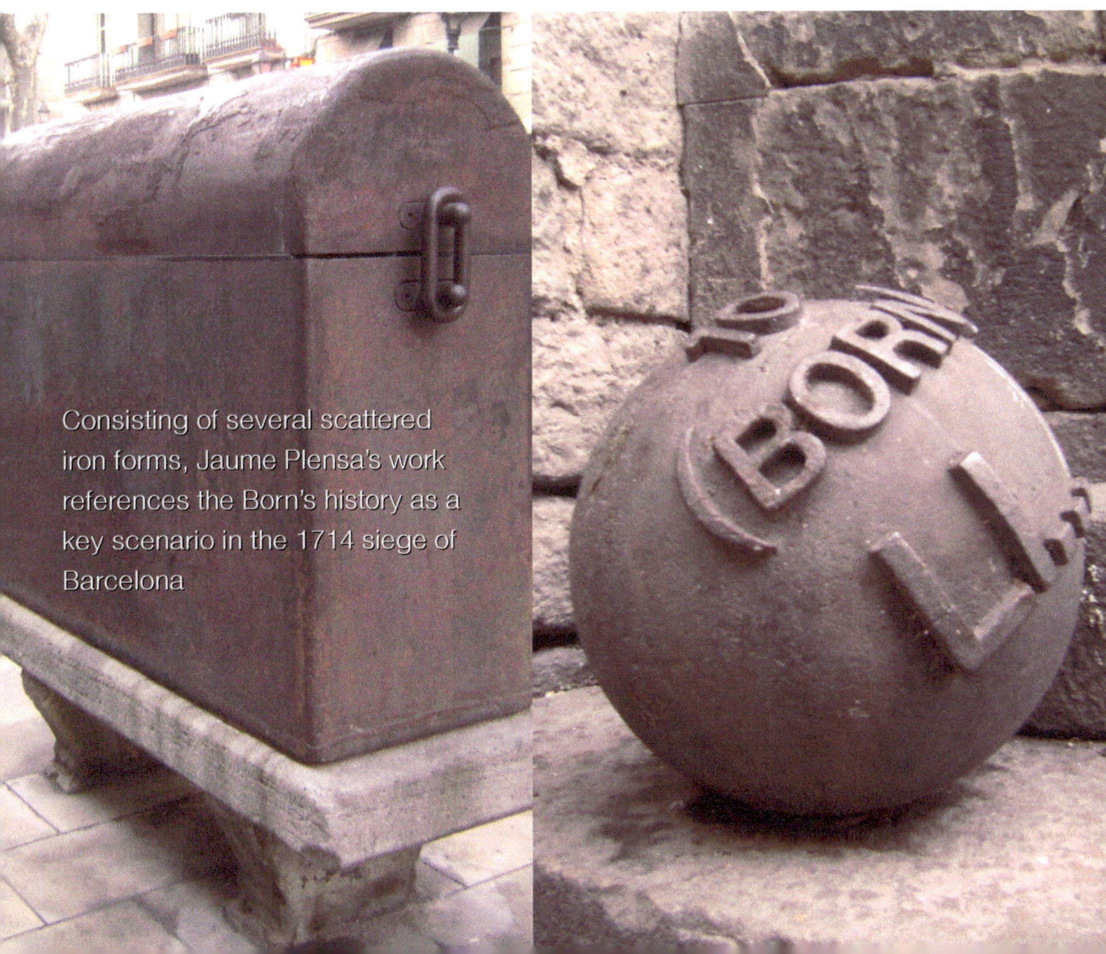

Consisting of several scattered iron forms, Jaume Plensa's work references the Born's history as a key scenario in the 1714 siege of Barcelona

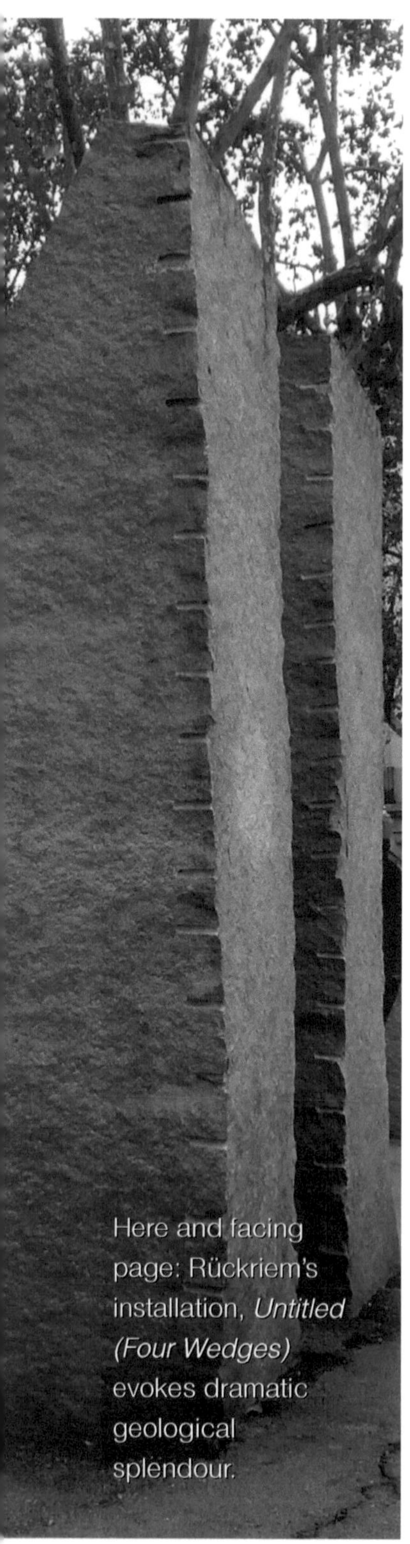

activated by a sensor that turns it on after dusk: around 6 pm in winter and 9 pm in summer.

Deuce Coop (1992) by James Turrell.. Neon installation. Centre Cívic Convent de Sant Agustí, Carrer Comerç, 36, La Ribera. Opening hours (after dusk): Monday to Friday, until 10 pm; Satur-days, until 9 pm.
Coordinates: *41.387659, 2.181615*

ii. *Born* by Jaume Plensa. Consisting of several scattered iron forms, including a large coffer and spheres resembling cannonballs, this work focusses attention on the urban landscape of the tree-lined avenue, evoking the form of a ship. However, it also references the Born's history as a Medieval jousting yard, the site of the main wholesale market and a key scenario in the 1714 siege when the city fell.
Under the defunct market structure—a sublime example of late-nineteenth-century ironwork—at the end of this avenue, archaeological excavations have revealed the original neighbourhood of 1714–1715. The site has been turned into a permanent exhibition. It is one of those times when paying a few euros' admission fee is worthwhile.

Born (1992) by Jaume Plensa. Iron. Passeig del Born/Volta d'en Dusai, Born. **Coordinates:** *41.384281, 2.182506*

Kevin Booth

iii. *Sense títol (quatre falques) / Untitled (Four Wedges)* by Ulrich Rückriem.

This Düsseldorf artist, trained as a stone mason, installed four massive pieces of granite in the Pla del Palau, distributed in two pairs, which face the traffic like spectators. While much of his work evokes dramatic geological splendour, here the setting is poor, causing many people to pass by, unseeing, as oblivious to the work as to any other element of urban furniture. It is a shame because the piece deserves more attention.

Sense títol (quatre falques) / Untitled (Four Wedges) (1992) by Ulrich Rückriem. Granite. Pla de Palau.
Coordinates: *41.382538, 2.183644*

For the following works, see the chapters ahead:

iv. *Rosa dels vents / Compass Rose*, (1992) by Lothar Baumgarten. Embedded bronze letters. Plaça Pau Vila, Moll de la Barceloneta.
Coordinates: *41.381383, 2.186168* to *41.379325, 2.186937*

v. *Crescendo appare / Growing in Appearance* (1992) by Mario Merz. Neon and glass. Plaça Pau Vila, Moll de la Barceloneta.
Coordinates: *41.376372, 2.187541* to *41.377711, 2.187846*

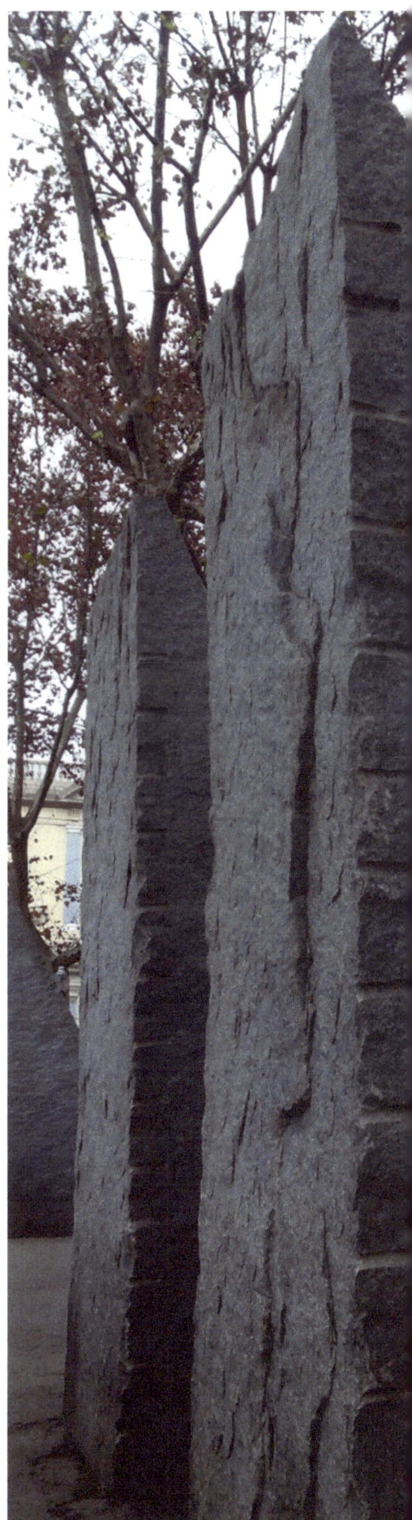

vi. *Una habitació on sempre plou / A Room Where It Is Always Raining* (1992) by Juan Muñoz. Iron and bronze. Plaça del Mar, Barceloneta.
Coordinates: *41.374854, 2.189277*

vii. *L'Estel ferit / The Wounded Star*, (1992) by Rebecca Horn. Glass and iron on a concrete plinth. Carrer Sant Miquel Platja, 8, Barceloneta.
Coordinates: *41.376497, 2.191080*

viii. *Balança romana / Roman Scales*, (1993) by Jannis Kounellis. Iron, sacking and coffee beans. Corner of Carrers Miquel Boera and Andrea Dòria, Barceloneta.
Coordinates: *41.380328, 2.192197*

References:

> *http://jamesturrell.com*
> *http://jaumeplensa.com*
> *http://www.tate.org.uk/art/artists/ulrich-ruckriem-2258*

The oculus in Turrell's installation is a hallmark of his work, as is his striking use of light.

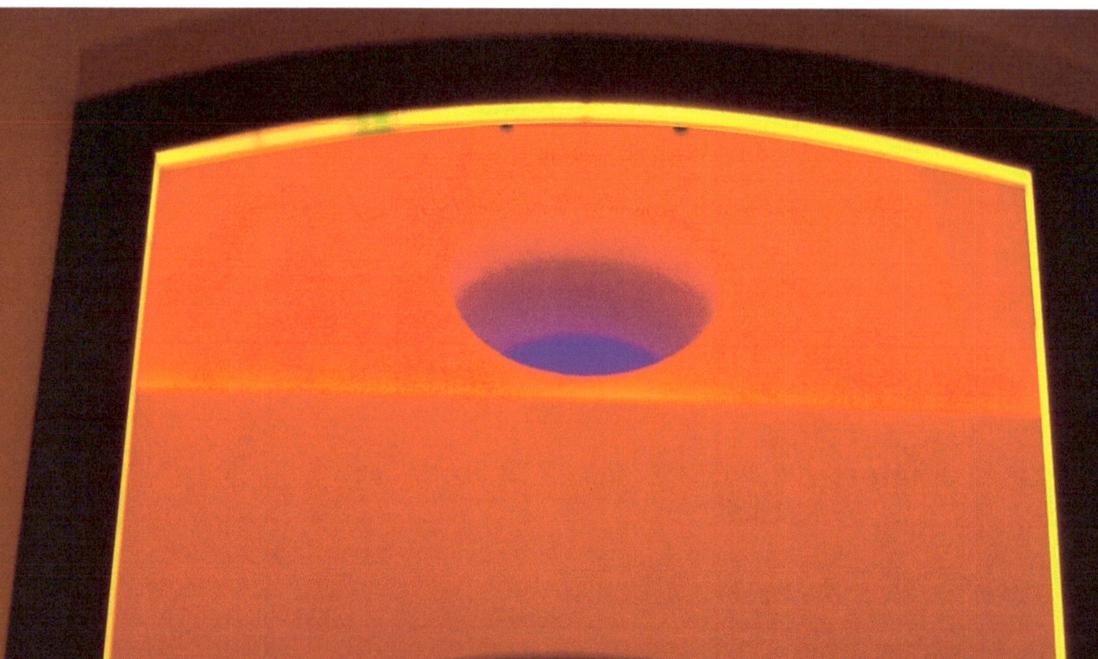

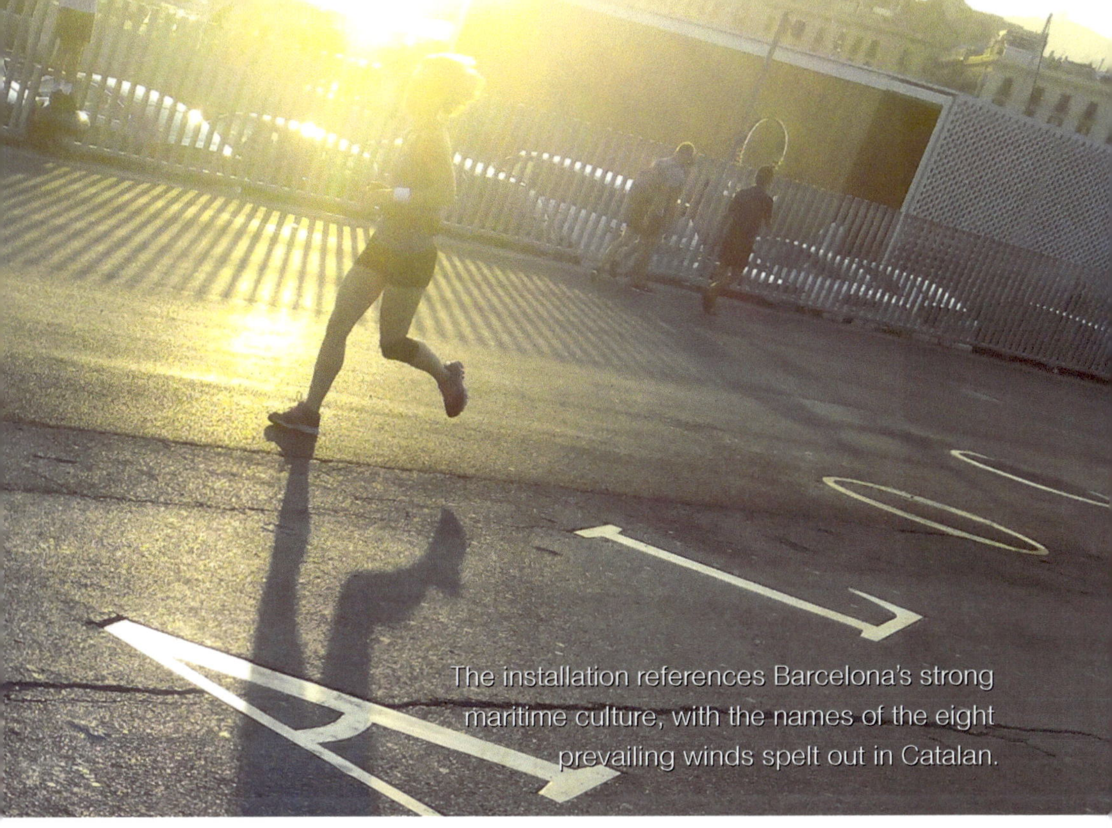

7. A compass rose

Lothar Baumgarten is a German sculptor and installation artist who lives between Berlin and New York. While not essentially a photographer, still photos and film are a favourite medium for framing his art. He was a student of Joseph Beuys, and likes to use names as signifiers in his installations to highlight ecological or historical issues such as colonial exploitation and cultural hegemony.

Rosa dels vents (Compass Rose) references Barcelona's strong maritime culture. It is a hard work to view as it extends over several hundred square metres on the Moll de la Barceloneta. Large bronze letters embedded in the pavement spell out in Catalan the names of the eight prevailing winds, indicating their direction. Though originally conceived to be placed geographically closer together, the area's architectural planners decided that the installation's

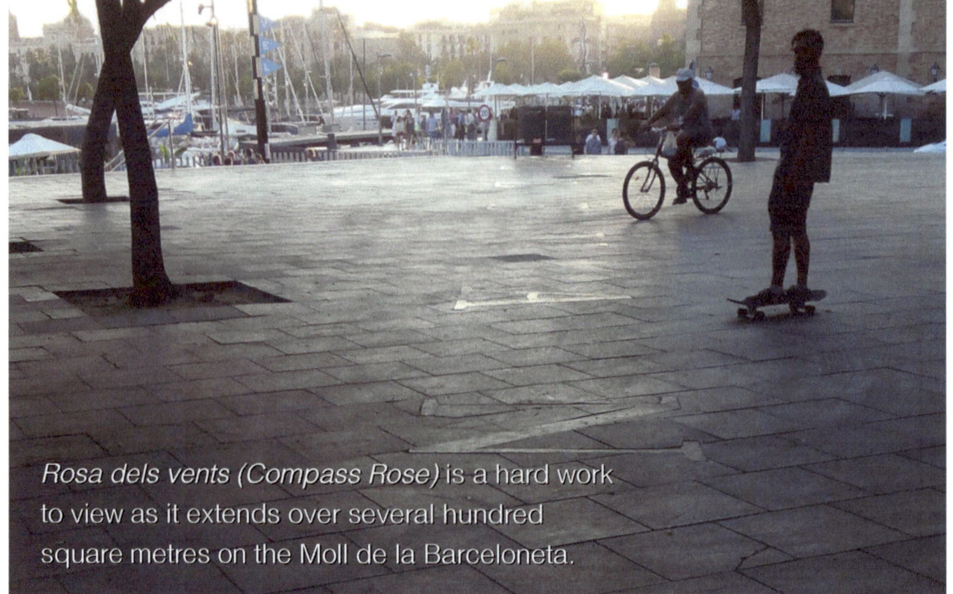

separate components would have more impact in their present arrangement. Look for them: *tramuntana* or port wind (N), *gregal* (NE), *llevant* (E), *xaloc* (SE), *migjorn* (S), *garbi* or *llebeig* (SW), *ponent* (W) and *mestral, cerc* or *serè* (NW).

Rosa dels vents is one of eight pieces comprising "Configuraciones urbanes" ("Urban Configurations"), a plural installation conceived to form a chain of artworks linking the neighbourhoods of La Ribera and Barceloneta, inaugurated for the 1992 Olympics.

Rosa dels vents / Compass Rose (1992) by Lothar Baumgarten. Embedded bronze letters. Plaça Pau Vila, Moll de la Barceloneta.
Coordinates: *41.381383, 2.186168* to *41.379325, 2.186937*

References:

http://www.tate.org.uk/art/artists/lothar-baumgarten-706

Kevin Booth

8.
The measure of a shell

Unsurprisingly, for this installation of cobble-embedded neon, Italian artist Mario Merz chose the Fibonacci sequence, a ratio occurring naturally in objects such as the nautilus shell. Though defined by various Indian mathematicians as early as 400 BCE and onwards, the formula received its name from an Italian, who defined the equation ($F_n = F_{n-1} + F_{n-2}$) in 1202. That means, starting from 0 and 1, you add the two previous numbers to find the next, producing the sequence: 0, 1, 1, 2, 3, 5, 8, 13, 21, 34, 55, 89, 144 …

This is another work in "Configuraciones urbanes" ("Urban Configurations"),

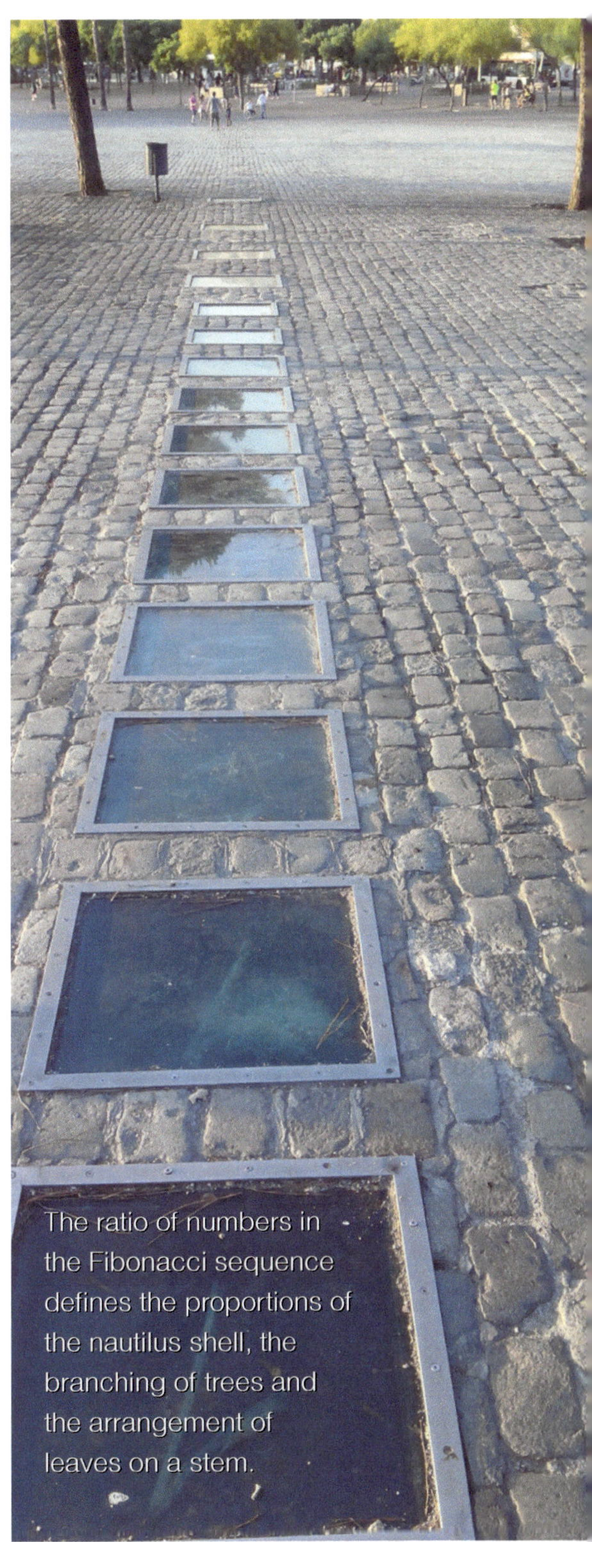
The ratio of numbers in the Fibonacci sequence defines the proportions of the nautilus shell, the branching of trees and the arrangement of leaves on a stem.

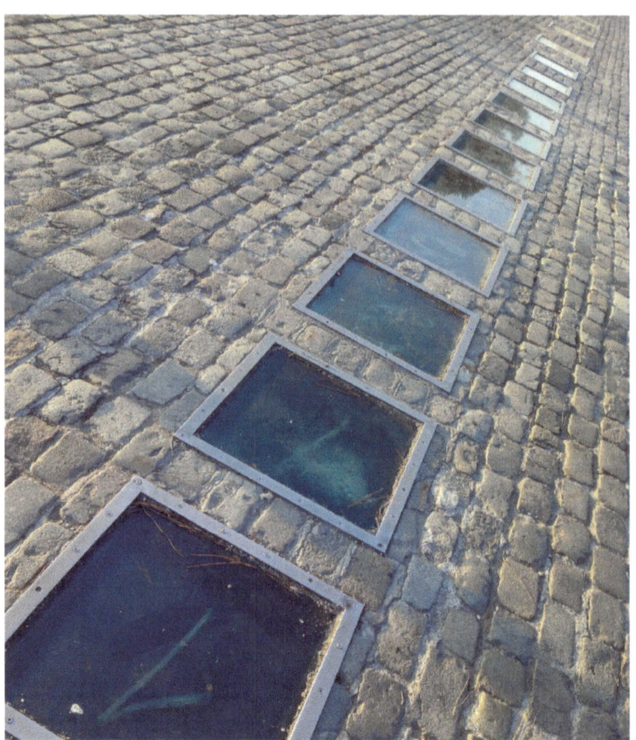

This sequence is much used in computer algorithms and is related to the so-called golden ratio, or approximately 1 to 1.618.

which stretches the length of the Moll de la Barceloneta. Each neon number in the sequence is protected in its own cavity under shockproof glass, arranged at the distance from its neighbours that corresponds to its position in the sequence. Is the concept of laying out the dimensions of a shell an attempt to reflect Barceloneta's close relationship to the sea? In fact, Merz used this sequence in much of his work, interpreting it to signify universal creation and growth. According to the Tate, which houses six of his pieces, he had "a fascination with the material and metaphorical qualities of natural objects with ideas regarding infinity and repetition".

Mario Merz (1925–2003) is an interesting artist. His father, an architect, taught him a sensitivity to the "human, intimate and natural" occupation of space. Later, he sank his roots into the passionate post-war scene of 1950s Turin. Here, he mixed with influential writers like Elio Vittorini (the communist author of *Conversations in Sicily*, an oneiric and

Kevin Booth

beguiling novel that is a coded criticism of fascism) and Ezra Pound (whose fascist and anti-semitic politics made him a controversial figure among English poets). Along with the sculptor Marisa Merz, who was also his wife, he was a key developer of *Arte Povera* (poor art), a movement that attacked the perceived establishment with an art using mundane and unconventional materials. Other international figures linked to this movement are the Greek artist Jannis Kounellis and the Catalan artists of the *Dau al Set* (seven-sided die) Movement, whose founders included Joan Brossa and Antoni Tàpies.

Crescendo appare / Growing in Appearance, Mario Merz, Plaça Pau Vila, Moll de la Barceloneta.
Coordinates: *41.376372, 2.187541* to *41.377711, 2.187846*

References:

http://www.tate.org.uk/art/artists/mario-merz-1623
http://www.theguardian.com/news/2003/nov/13/guardia
nobituaries.italy

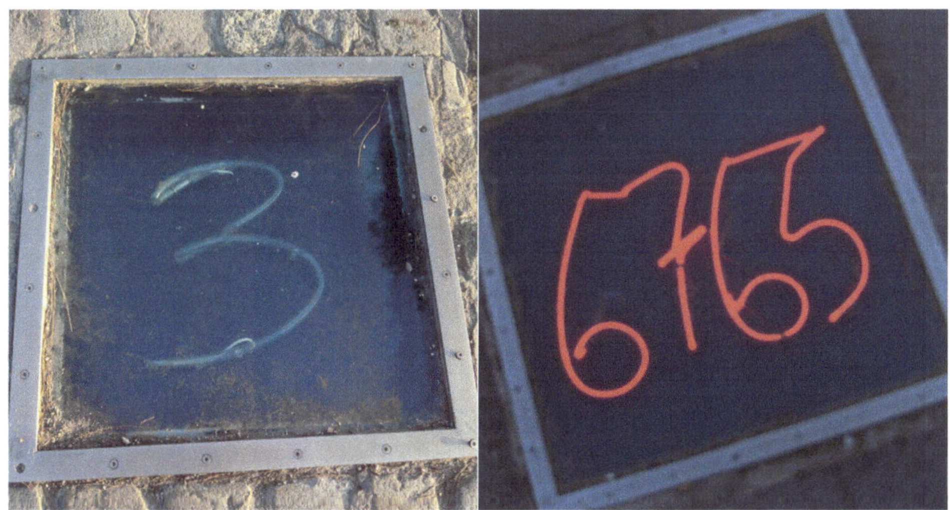

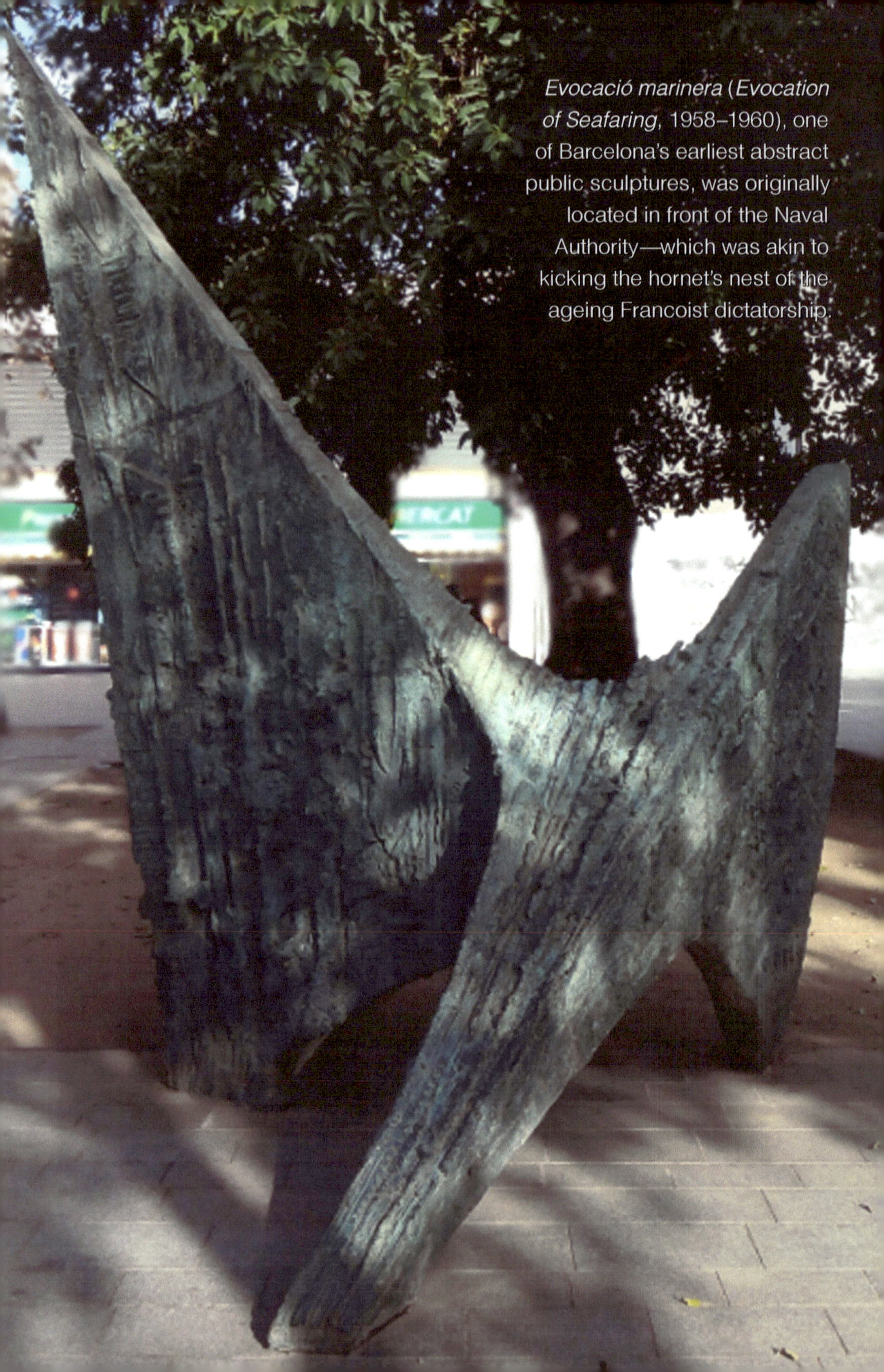

Evocació marinera (*Evocation of Seafaring*, 1958–1960), one of Barcelona's earliest abstract public sculptures, was originally located in front of the Naval Authority—which was akin to kicking the hornet's nest of the ageing Francoist dictatorship.

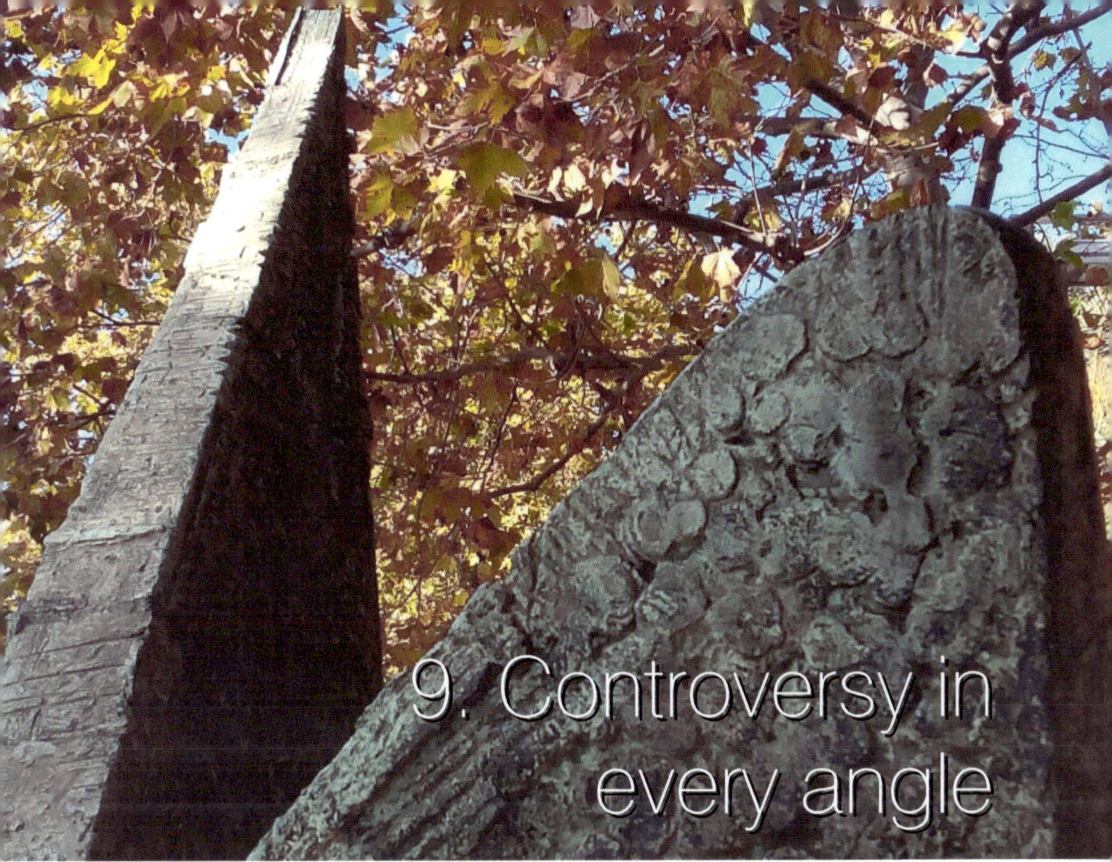

Alongside Tàpies, Picasso and Miró, Josep Maria Subirachs (1927–2014) stands as one of Spain's most important twentieth-century artists. His seventy or so sculptures scattered around Barcelona include a *Homage to Francesc Macià* (known as Catalonia's grandfather) and the Passion façade of the Sagrada Família Temple. Surprisingly, of these four artists, he is the only one not to have his own foundation or museum in Barcelona, after the private gallery, Espai Regomir, which had displayed much of his small-format *oeuvre*, had to close in 2014 due to a bylaw that cancelled its permanent lease. The savings bank Fundació Caixa Penedès was to have rehabilitated the parish church of Sant Cugat del Rec in Carrer Princesa as a museum for his work, but the recession forced the project to be abandoned in 2011.

Subirachs began his sculptural career as an adept of Noucentisme (nine-hundred-ism)—named by Eugeni d'Ors in Italianate fashion after the century (e.g. 1400–1499 is

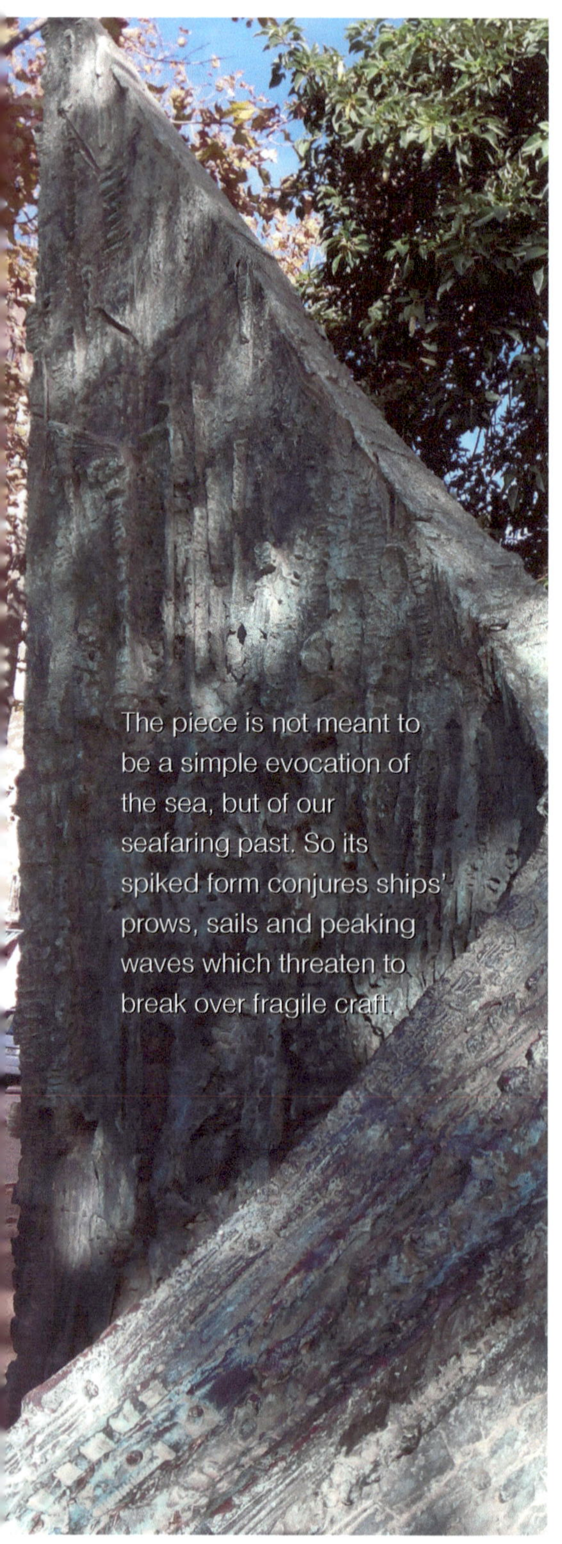

known as Quattrocento). "Nou" means both "nine" and "new" in Catalan, and Noucentisme was a guiding stylistic force for the first three decades of the twentieth century in Catalonia. The movement sought to counter the excesses of Modernisme's effusiveness and fantasy with cool Neo-Classical balance. Many of the spaces created for Barcelona's 1929 World's Fair, such as Plaça Catalunya, Plaça Espanya and the landscaping of Montjuïc are the result of this impetus.

So it is unsurprising that Subirachs, born in 1927, should have first been inspired by such Noucentista sculptors as Josep Clarà i Ayats. In fact, Subirachs was to incorporate Clarà i Ayats' *La deessa* (*The Goddess*) into his *Monument a Francesc Macià* (*Monument to Francesc Macià*) in Plaça Catalunya in 1991.

Subirachs began in a strongly Noucentista figurative style. Nevertheless, by the mid-fifties, his work was becoming progressively abstract, experimenting with the angular, erotic forms and haunting vacuums that invert

Kevin Booth

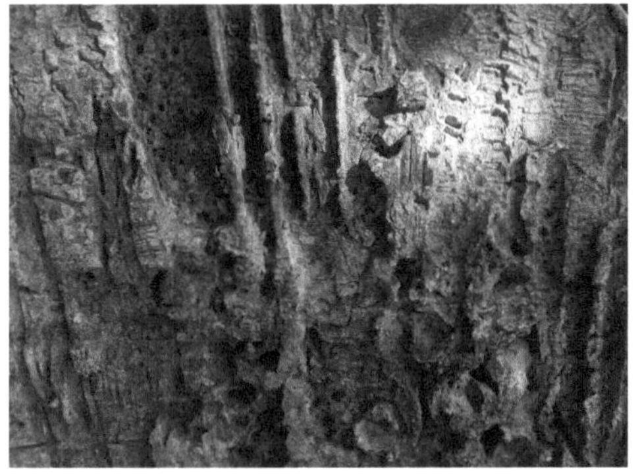

The sculpture's surface texture recalls the degradation of bleached timbers, rotted by the elements.

the human volumes, evoking visual paradoxes, midway between architectural elements and organic creations, which would be a hallmark of his work on the Sagrada Família.

His leap into full-on abstraction—a development that, while well underway beyond Spain's borders, represented nothing less than profanity to the tightly controlled, Neo-Classical aesthetic of Francoist Spain—came with *Forma 212* (*Form 212*, 1957), the first abstract sculpture to be displayed publicly in Barcelona. It is installed outside Llars Mundet, close to Joan Brossa's *Accessible Visual Poem in Three Tenses: birth, journey—with pauses and intonations —and destruction.*

Being fairly well out of the public eye, that sculpture ducked any controversy; so it was his second abstract work, *Evocation of Seafaring*, begun in 1958, which attracted the ire of the conservatives. The piece was originally located at the bottom of the Ramblas in front of the Navy Headquarters—which was akin to kicking the hornet's nest of the ageing Francoist dictatorship, so it was soon moved to its current site.

The piece is not meant to be a simple evocation of the sea, but of our seafaring past. Hence it aims to do more than just replicate marine motifs but rather pay tribute to human beings' fight for survival in and dominance of this vital environment. So its spiked forms evoke ships' prows, sails and peaking waves that threaten to break over fragile craft, while the sculpture's surface texture recalls the degradation of bleached timbers, rotted by the elements.

Controversy was a current against which Subirachs swam throughout his career, and other conflicts followed the fury generated by those first abstract sculptures. Throughout the sixties, he was active in protests against the Franco dictatorship, contributing with the creation of a medal commemorating the founding of the Sindicat Democràtic d'Estudiants de la Universitat de Barcelona (Democratic Student Union of the University of Barcelona), a union of students and professors against the dictatorship, to help pay the fines and court cases that its members faced after a police siege (known as the "caputxinada") in 1966.

From 1987 onwards he began to live, as had Gaudí, on-site at the Sagrada Família, where he had been commissioned to create the Passion façade. In 1990, the art magazine *Arctus* discovered, the night before the publication of one of its issues, it had an entire blank page unaccounted for, and therefore decided to run an article decrying the manner in which Subirachs' contribution to the Temple was defacing Gaudí's work.

It should be stressed that Subirachs' work on the Sagrada Família at that time signified the largest sculptural assembly of any living artist in the world. Though he had planned to dedicate fifteen years to this last major work of his life, he finally devoted over twenty-three, during which time he assiduously studied the New Testament, despite his religious ambivalence.

But the storm clouds gathered apace. The next morning, Subirachs peered out from the scaffolding around the Temple to observe a quasi-religious procession traipsing about the holy site in protest at his sculptural offerings. When asked years later whether the criticism had affected him, his response was:

> *"Things don't happen for no reason. [The criticisms] made me more attentive. I said to myself: 'Hey, this is something to which everyone pays attention, even those who are against me and are capable of organising a campaign.' That meant that I was always*

     Kevin Booth

more lucid, wide awake. I believe I'm doing something that people see and have an opinion on, so I have to look at it even more carefully."

In a late addendum to that protest, one of Subirachs' elements on the temple—a sculpted lion that had attracted scathing critical attention—was quietly removed in 2015. The Temple's management stated it was an apprentice's poorly executed work, but Subirachs' critics (who are legion) claim otherwise. The irony of this story is that, in 1965, Subirachs had himself been a signatory to a petition arguing that contemporary work on the Sagrada Família was destroying Gaudí's original genius.

Subirachs' battles may have been largely a result of his lack of diplomacy concerning his fellow artists. For example, he endeared himself to few when he made a comment about Tàpies—possibly one of the world's

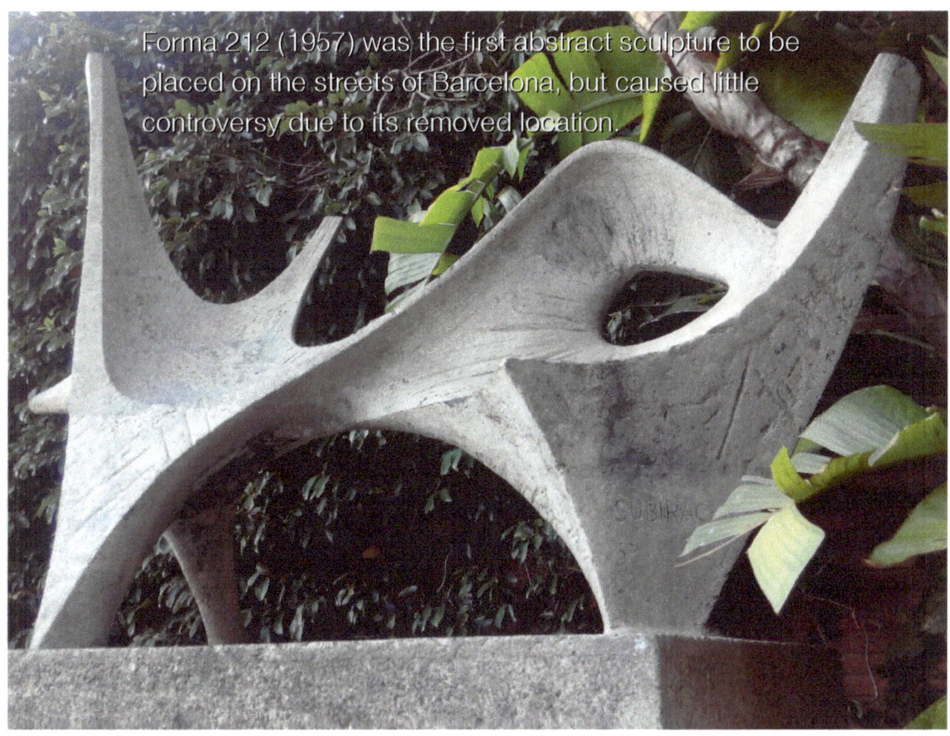

twentieth-century greats—and specifically, his *Monument to Picasso*:

> *"Definitely, [there are doubtful sculptures]. For example, one that I find horrible and seems strange to me that they have made is the* Monument to Picasso. *Furthermore, its upkeep costs huge amounts and I truly don't know what you can conserve from it."*

In the same interview, he said of Roy Lichtenstein's *Barcelona's Head*:

> *"Yes, he's an American painter, who is famous as a painter, but I don't believe he's ever made sculpture. But, in the end, he sent a design and they're creating it."*

Such flippant derision towards his contemporaries caused many of Barcelona's foremost art critics to turn their backs on this *enfant terrible*, which, in a small city like Barcelona, may have made his millstone somewhat heavier. Nevertheless, Subirachs is undoubtedly one of the heavyweights of twentieth-century Catalan art, so one can only hope that in the future he will regain his former higher standing.

Evocació Marinera / Evocation of Seafaring (1958–1960) by Josep Maria Subirachs. Bronze. Plaça del Mar, Barceloneta.

Coordinates: *41.375353, 2.189111*

Forma 212 / Form 212 (1957) by Josep Maria Subirachs. Concrete. Av. d'Arturo Mundet, s/n.
Coordinates: *41.435596, 2.147120*

References:
> *www.subirachs.cat*

     Kevin Booth

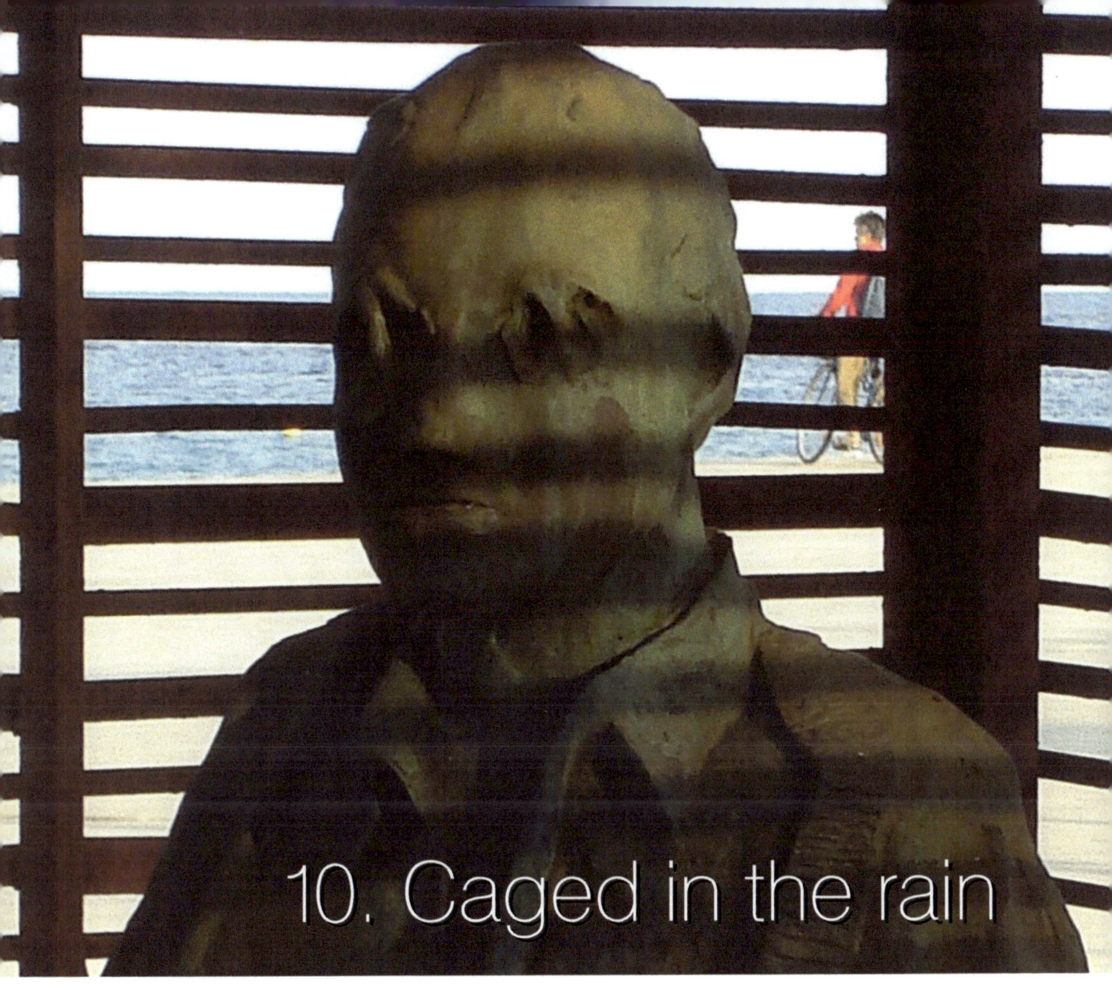

10. Caged in the rain

I n the same square, Plaça del Mar, you find another of the "Configuracions urbanes" ("Urban Configurations") pieces. This open square that serves as the main gateway onto the beach is the site of a rusty iron cage protected by five spreading trees. *Una habitació on sempre plou (A Room Where It Is Always Raining)* by the Madrid artist Juan Muñoz is also from that magic year, 1992.

Each of the five bronze figures inhabiting this double-arched aviary-like structure appears to grow from and remain rooted to a heavy semi-spherical base. Only a few details of clothing differentiate their anonymous yet virtually identical forms. Despite their strong sense of group, however, they appear curiously, almost wilfully oblivious to each other, consciously distant—as if expending enormous amounts of energy to avoid seeing the bars of their cell, or

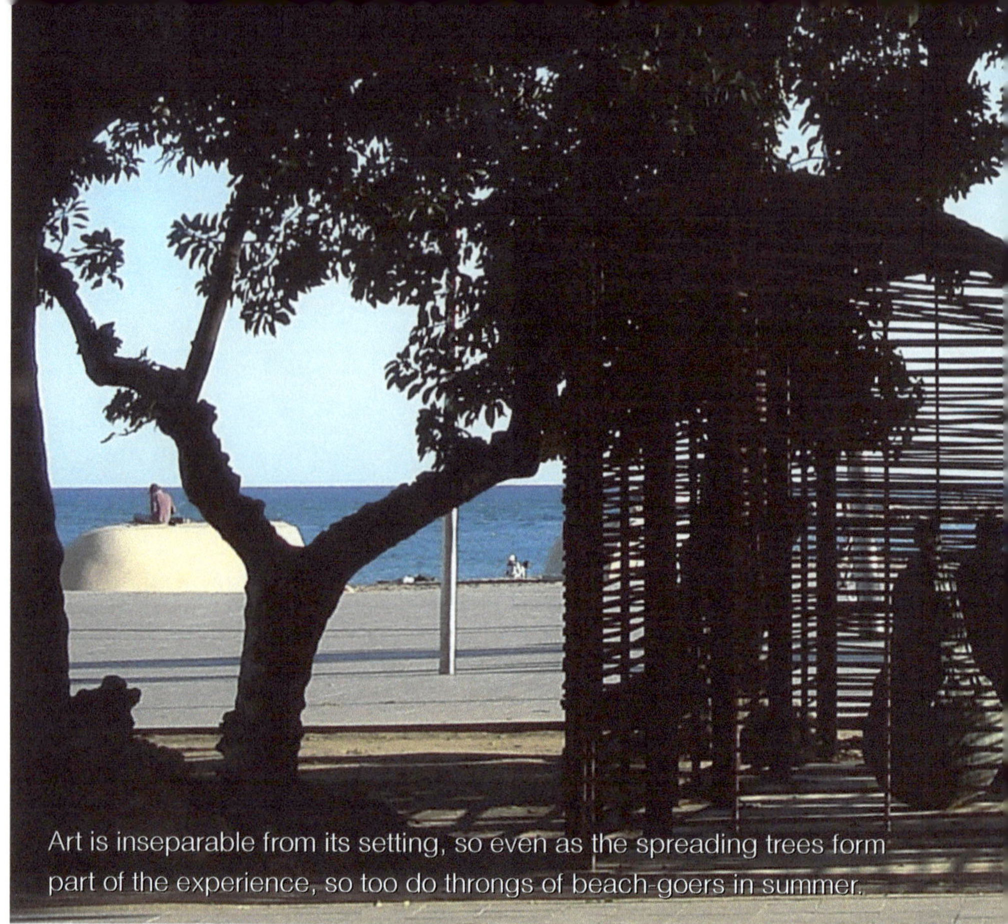

Art is inseparable from its setting, so even as the spreading trees form part of the experience, so too do throngs of beach-goers in summer.

their fellow inmates. This concurrent unity and disparity of Muñoz's figures evoke a group of political prisoners estranged by ideological differences. Their gazes never quite connect with any point, either outward, or with each other. Apparently the installation was meant to include water so that "rain" would perpetually fall into the cage; however, technical problems meant this feature was never implemented. Art is as much about its accidents as its intentions.

At around the time he produced this piece, Muñoz was beginning to work with "narrative" installations, using figures only slightly smaller than life-size that were engaged in interaction. His installations invite viewers in, to interact, even to discreetly take part. Among other media, Muñoz wrote short narrative pieces. He published "The Face of Pirandello" in *Urban Configurations*, the book that came out in 1994, two years after the exhibition:

                          Kevin Booth

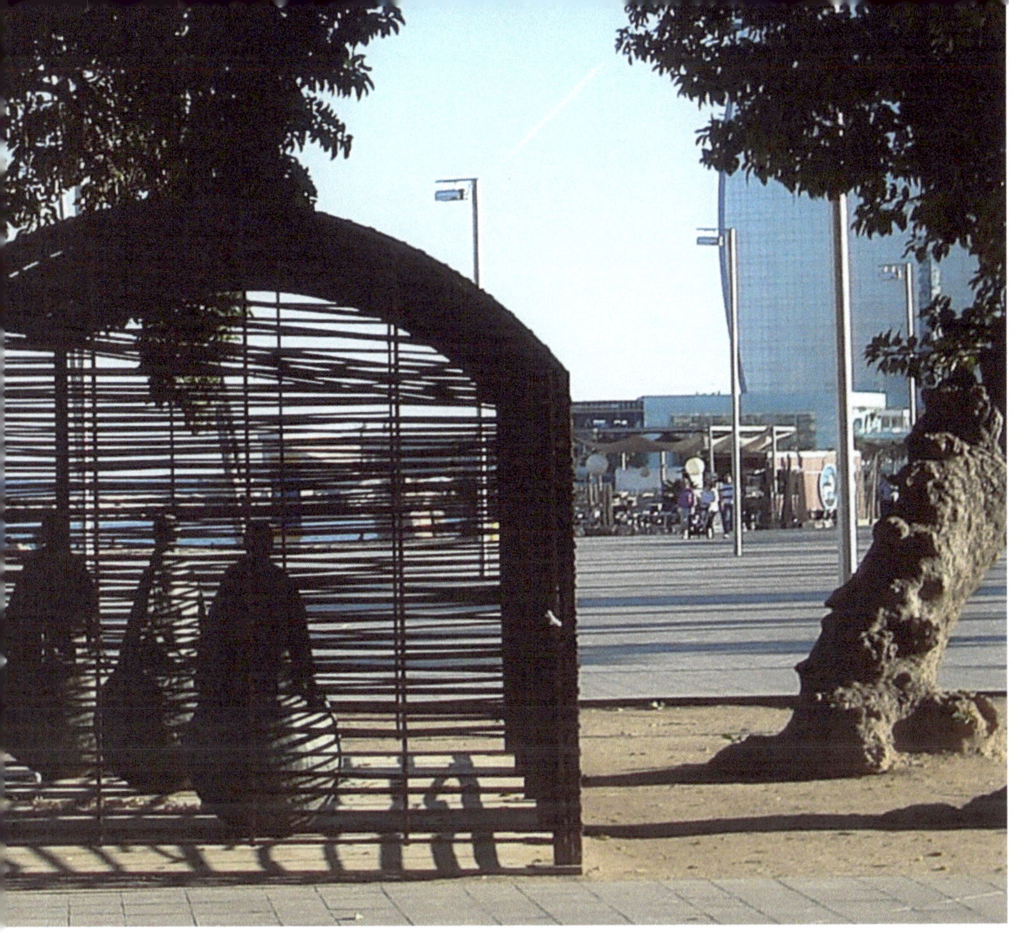

Allow me an image: the image of the face of Luigi Pirandello. Now allow me a second image that might explain the first: the image of a man who over a period of months buys several books by Pirandello. At first, he does so just to browse through his dramatic works. Later he purchases a few more books, this time not by Pirandello but about Pirandello. Perhaps to eye the framework. As the weeks go by, every time he takes one of the books from the shelf or puts it back, he stares for a few seconds at the face on the front and back covers of the books. As he goes from the shelf to the table and back again, his attention begins to become fixed, time after time, on the hat the Italian playwright wears in all his photographs.

Whatever the image of Pirandello's hat evokes, it nevertheless highlights one of the essential processes of

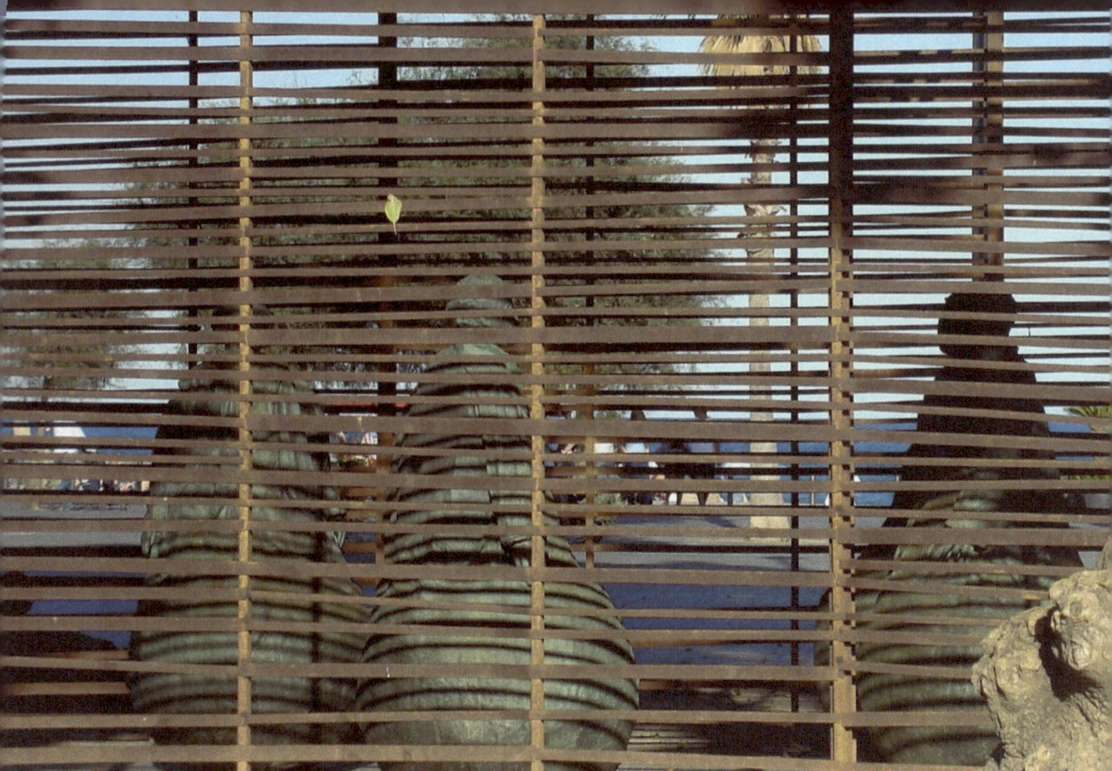

The installation was meant to include water so that "rain" would perpetually fall into the cage, however, technical problems meant this feature was never implemented.

viewing art. First comes the impact, of an image, sound effect or other sensory perception. You interact with, even become obsessed with the image for its own sake—its form, colour, composition or subject matter. Then secondary questions overtake the primary ones: how and why override the what. Juan Muñoz forces you to ask "What am I looking at here? What does it mean?" The image above of unseeing political prisoners is only an interpretation, as valid as any other yet also just as erroneous.

The placing of such a dour installation in the midst of this tourist beachfront might seem misplaced or at best ironic, but art is inseparable from its setting, so even as the spreading trees form part of the experience, so too do the bikini-clad throngs.

So that which is not art is an integral part of art, as Muñoz experienced here:

                    Kevin Booth

Among his earliest and surprisingly mature pieces were his balcony works: statues installed high on the wall of the exhibition chamber, which thereby transformed the space into an artwork in its own right.

In addition to the plastic arts, Muñoz was interested in atmospheric sound pieces, such as the BBC Radio 3

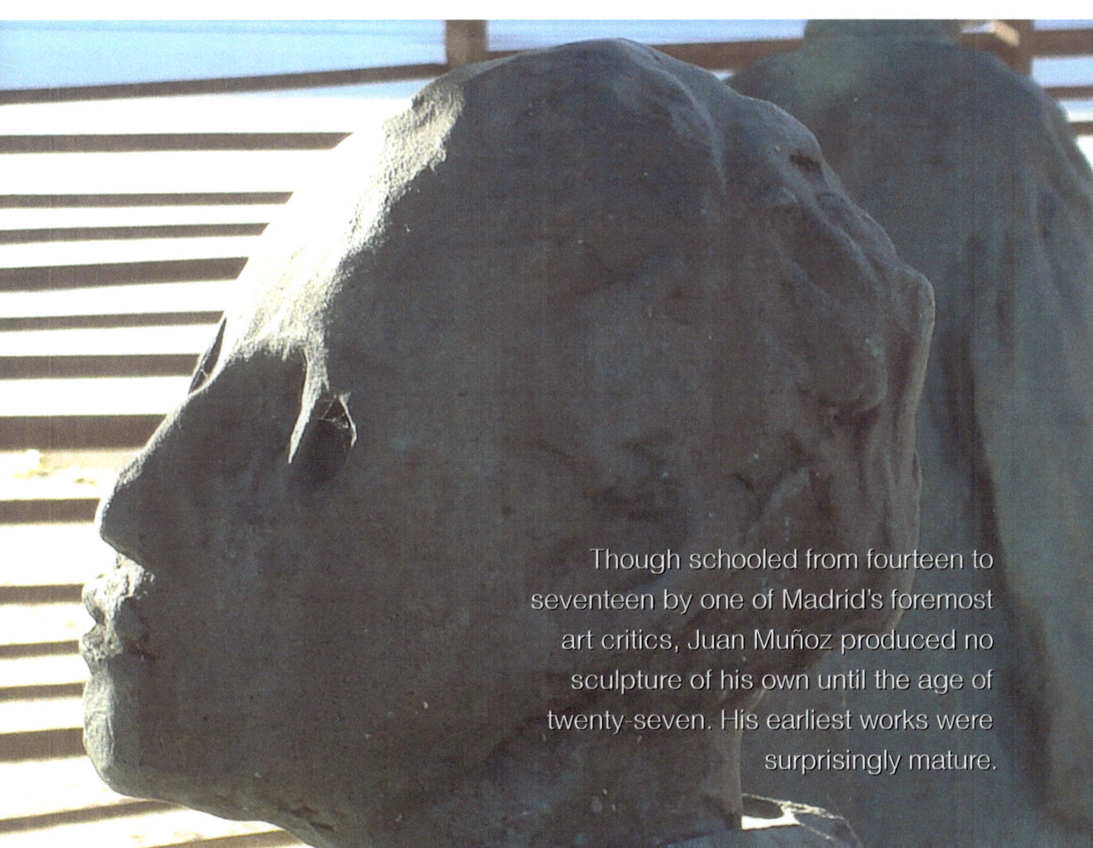

commission he created in collaboration with British composer Gavin Bryars, *A Man in a Room, Gambling* (1992). He won the National Spanish Prize for Plastic Arts in 2000, but died of a heart attack in Ibiza just one year later, aged 48. At that time an exhibition of his was being shown at London's Tate Gallery. His work can be found in the Museo Nacional Centro de Arte Reina Sofía, as well as in other Spanish and international collections.

Una habitació on sempre plou / A Room Where It Is Always Raining, Juan Muñoz, 1992. Plaça del Mar, Barceloneta.
Coordinates: *41.374854, 2.189277*

References:
   http://juanmunozestate.org/
   http://www.hangarbicocca.org/events/a-man-in-a-room-gambling/
   A revealing interview with Muñoz:
   http://press.uchicago.edu/Misc/Chicago/042901.html
   Configuracions urbanes (print edition), Moure, Gloria. Edicions Polígrafa, Barcelona, 1994.

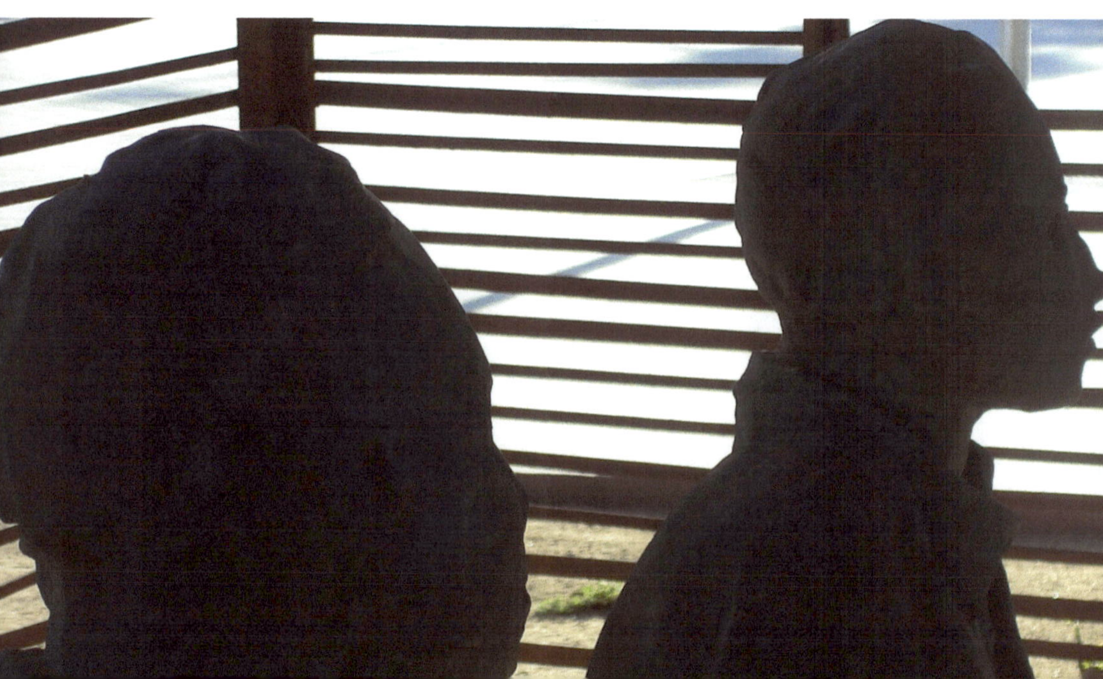

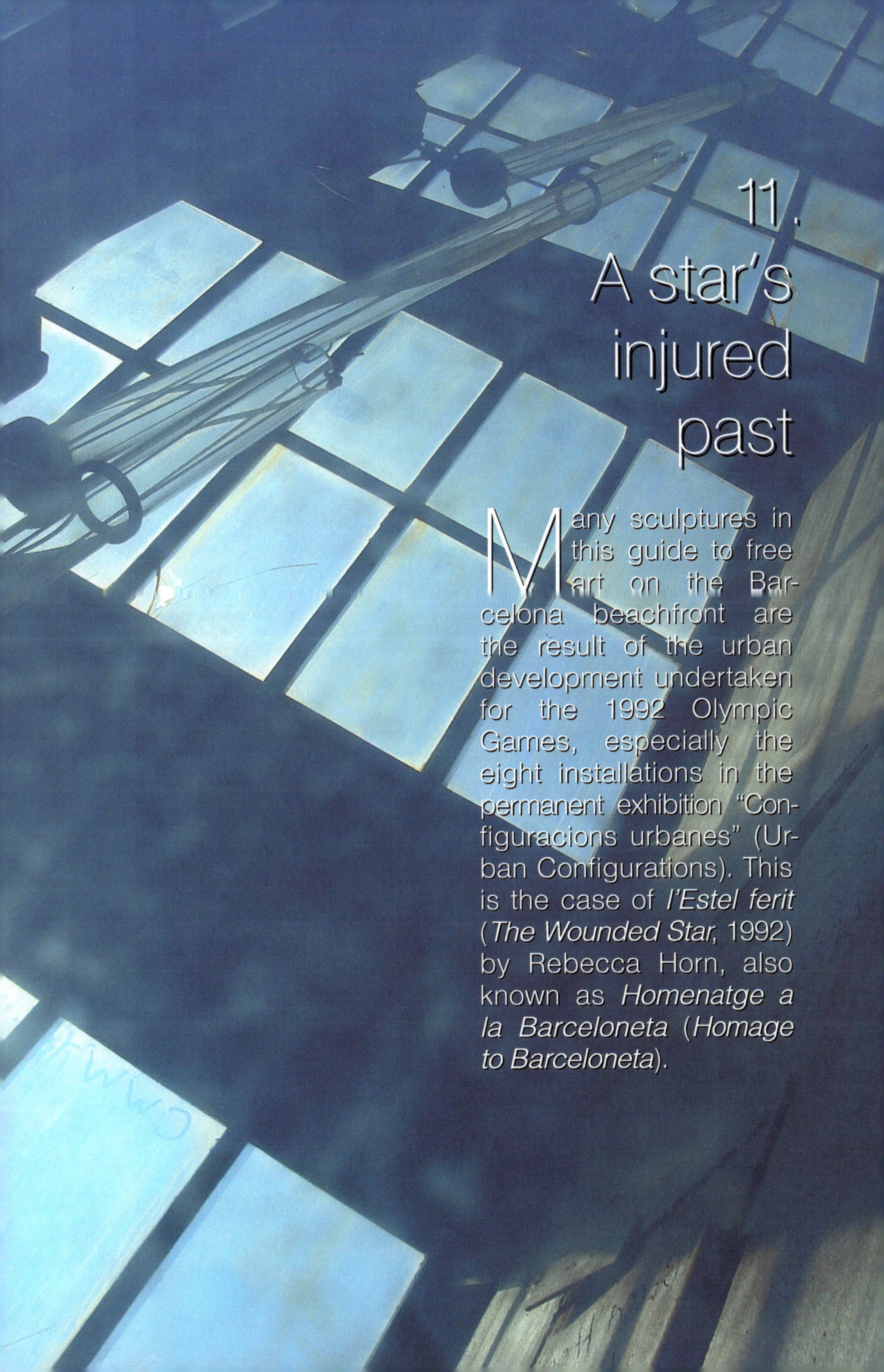

11.
A star's injured past

Many sculptures in this guide to free art on the Barcelona beachfront are the result of the urban development undertaken for the 1992 Olympic Games, especially the eight installations in the permanent exhibition "Configuracions urbanes" (Urban Configurations). This is the case of *l'Estel ferit* (*The Wounded Star*, 1992) by Rebecca Horn, also known as *Homenatge a la Barceloneta* (*Homage to Barceloneta*).

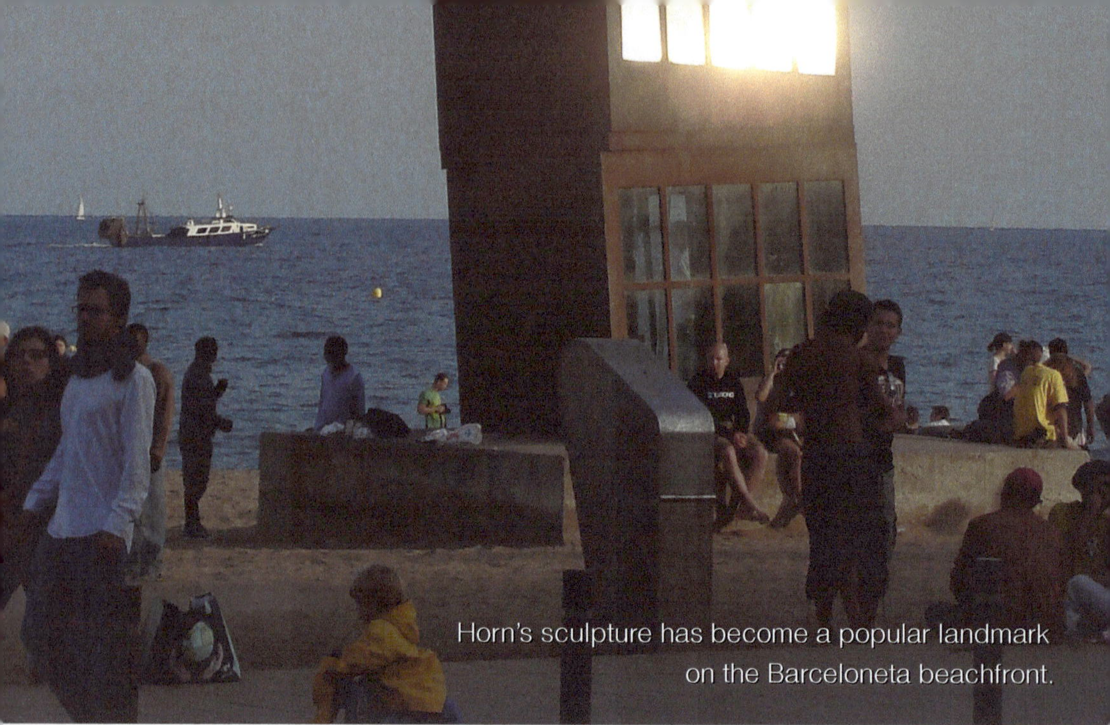

Horn's sculpture has become a popular landmark on the Barceloneta beachfront.

The piece consists of four large iron boxes piled up into a crooked tower like an abandoned lighthouse (dimensions: 10.60 x 5.17 x 5.17 m). The installation recalls aspects of Barceloneta's historical development from an artificial sand spit into a densely inhabited metropolitan area. It mimics the rational, geometric layout of low-rise buildings imposed by military engineer Juan Martín de Cermeño in 1753, roughly following the plan of his predecessor Joris Prosper van Verboom after the conquest of Barcelona in 1714. The plan was that residents displaced from La Ribera neighbourhood would be relocated here due to the construction of the Ciutadella fortress, but this never occurred. Instead, the authorities, wishing to impose order on this rapidly expanding fishing and port community, gave priority to those with sea-related occupations.

The installation's salt-encrusted windows reveal an internal mast-like structure that evokes the area's maritime past. It also recalls a former time of ramshackle beachfront restaurants (defying all health or building regulations with anarchist bravado) that once extended their tables right down onto the sand and were popular Sunday eateries

Kevin Booth

even as late as 1990. The mast carries neon tubes to light up the sculpture at night and, when working, is supposed to play recordings of softly speaking voices.

This piece stems from Horn's own experience of living in Barceloneta:

> *"In 1964 I was 20 years old and living in Barcelona, in one of those hotels where you rent rooms by the hour. I was working with fibreglass, without a mask, because nobody said it was dangerous, and I got very sick."*

As a result, she spent a year in hospital, during which time her parents died, furthering her sense of isolation. Perhaps the piece's title is a reference to this time. During her long recovery she had to abandon fibreglass in favour of softer materials and drawing tools. The changes that these constrictions forced upon her work led to her well-known body sculptures in pieces such as *Unicorn* (1970–1972) or *Pencil Mask* (1972), and also to creating cocoon-like creations such as

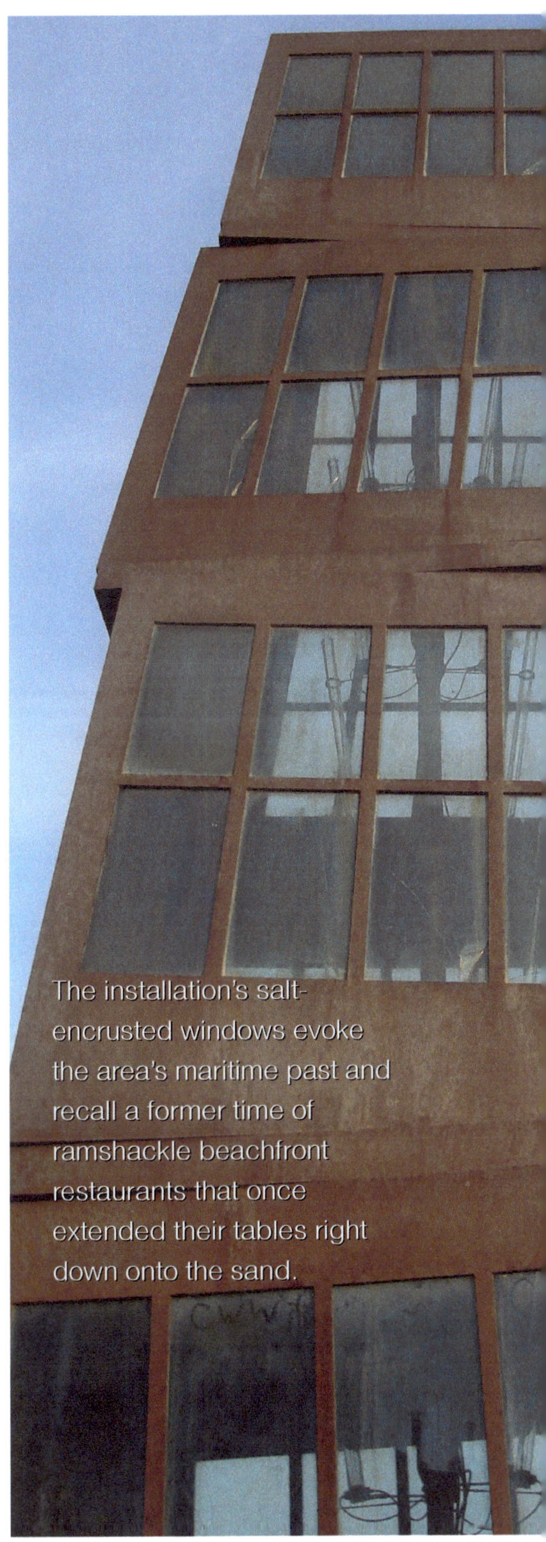

The installation's salt-encrusted windows evoke the area's maritime past and recall a former time of ramshackle beachfront restaurants that once extended their tables right down onto the sand.

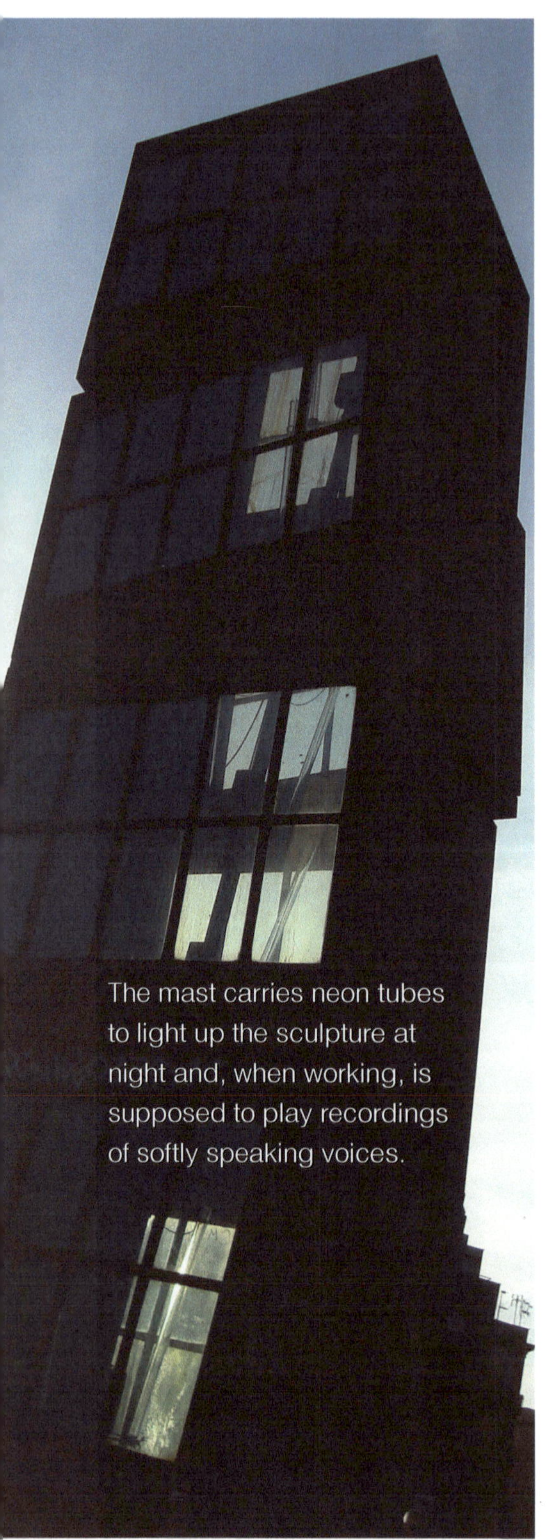

The mast carries neon tubes to light up the sculpture at night and, when working, is supposed to play recordings of softly speaking voices.

The Feathered Prison Fan (1978), using materials like feathers, balsa wood and cloth. Later works such as *Concert for Anarchy* (1990), on display at the Tate, play on absurdity and a violent tension contained within everyday objects.

L'Estel ferit / The Wounded Star (1992) by Rebecca Horn. Carrer Sant Miquel Platja, 8, Barceloneta.

Coordinates: *41.376497, 2.191080*

References:

*http://www.rebecca-horn.de
http://www.tate.org.uk/art/artworks/horn-concert-for-anarchy-t07517*

   Kevin Booth

12. The balance of trade in Barceloneta

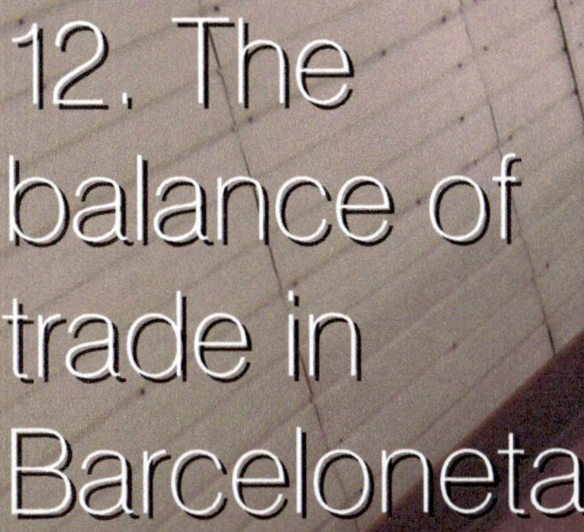

Jannis Kounellis, though Greek, was at one time, like Mario Merz, an exponent of Italy's Arte Povera (poor art) Movement. This late-sixties movement used humble materials and found objects—in a similar way to the Catalan artists of the *Dau al Set* (seven-sided die) group, founded by Joan Brossa and Antoni Tàpies—to create an art of protest that attacked the conservative establishment.

So Kounellis's materials were often raw and basic – iron, sacking, wool and cotton– and this impetus led to growing experimentation with bizarre materials such as fire and soot, to the point where in 1969, in a much-criticised show, he tethered twelve live horses in Rome's Galleria L'Attico. The aim

—through the juxtaposition of these archetypically traditional and rustic (not to mention live) elements in a pristine, cosmopolitan gallery space—was to make a statement on the fragmentation of modern life.

The work you see here, *Balança romana* (*Roman Scales*), is another of the pieces in the 1992 permanent exhibition "Urban Configurations". As Lothar Baumgarten intended with *Compass Rose* and Rebecca Horn with *The Wounded Star*, Kounellis is paying homage to Barceloneta's trading and maritime history. The work consists of a vertical conveyor, or weighing scales, containing sacks of coffee beans, rising to the height of the seven-storey building against which the piece is installed. By using coffee beans—an everyday staple of early twentieth-century Barcelona life, one that would have been unloaded at the port and yet which hails from exotic, often colonised locations like South America—Kounellis is foregrounding issues such as trade, exploitation and colonialism. His sculptures are characteristically found in the historic, often industrial, locations that they reference, as in this case: Barceloneta was formerly a neighbourhood of dock workers and fishermen.

Kounellis's use of base materials, such as iron, sacking and coffee beans, reflects his roots in the Arte Povera (poor art) Movement, where everyday and found objects were employed to critique the capitalist establishment.

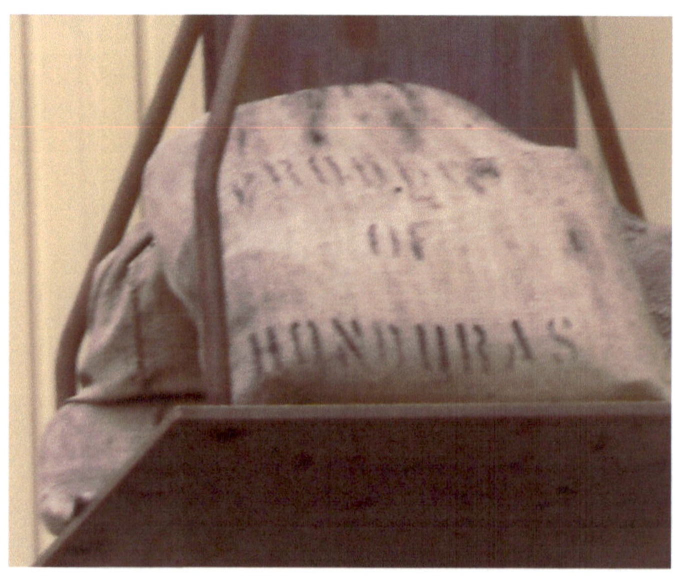

Kevin Booth

Apart from sculpture, Kounellis's work spans painting and performance. In one oil work (*Untitled*, 1971), in which he applied the Cubist device of painting musical notes on a flat canvas—in this case Bach's oratorio, the *St John Passion* —he also allowed for a cellist to play alongside the work, thereby 'activating' the piece.

Originally installed on the corner of Barceloneta's Baluard and Almirall Cervera streets, this sculpture now lives outside the community centre where Carrer Miquel Boera meets Andrea Dòria.

Balança romana / Roman Scales, Jannis Kounellis, 1993. Corner of Carrers Miquel Boera and Andrea Dòria, Barceloneta.

Coordinates: *41.380328, 2.192197*

References:

http://www.cheimread.com/ar tists/jannis-kounellis
http://www.tate.org.uk/art/arti sts/jannis-kounellis-1438

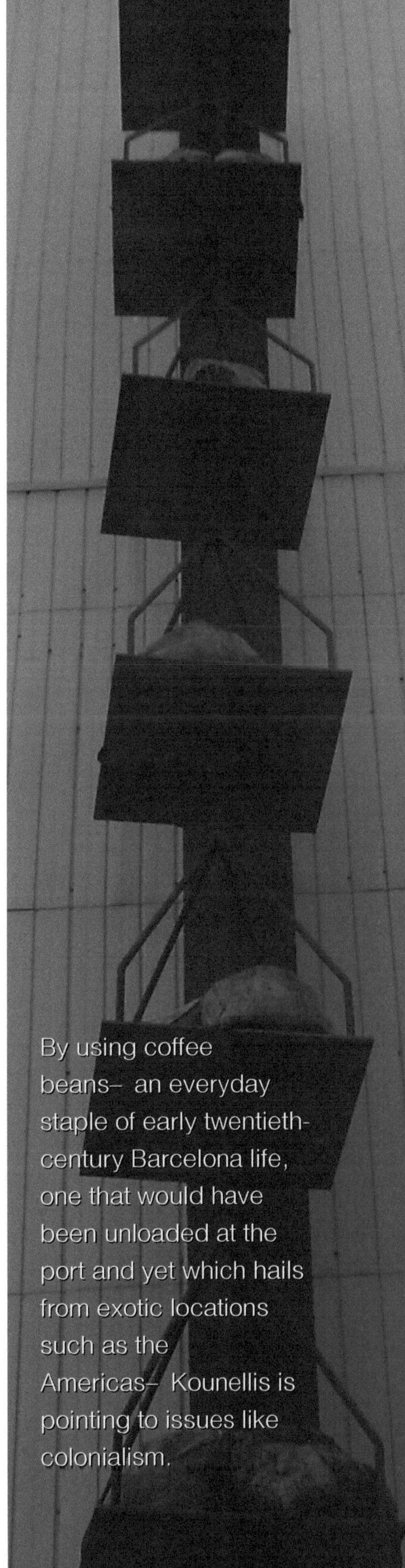

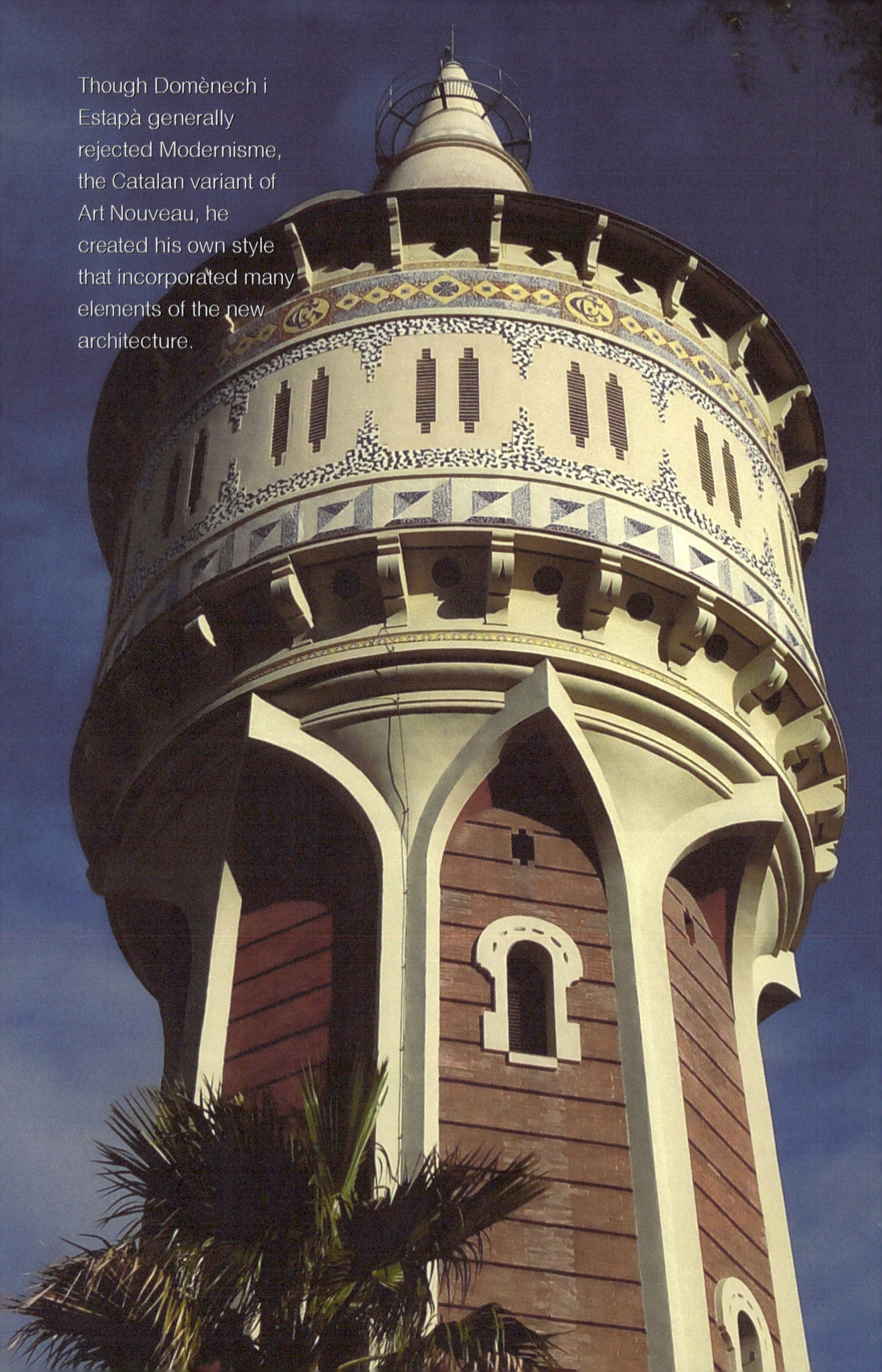

Though Domènech i
Estapà generally
rejected Modernisme,
the Catalan variant of
Art Nouveau, he
created his own style
that incorporated many
elements of the new
architecture.

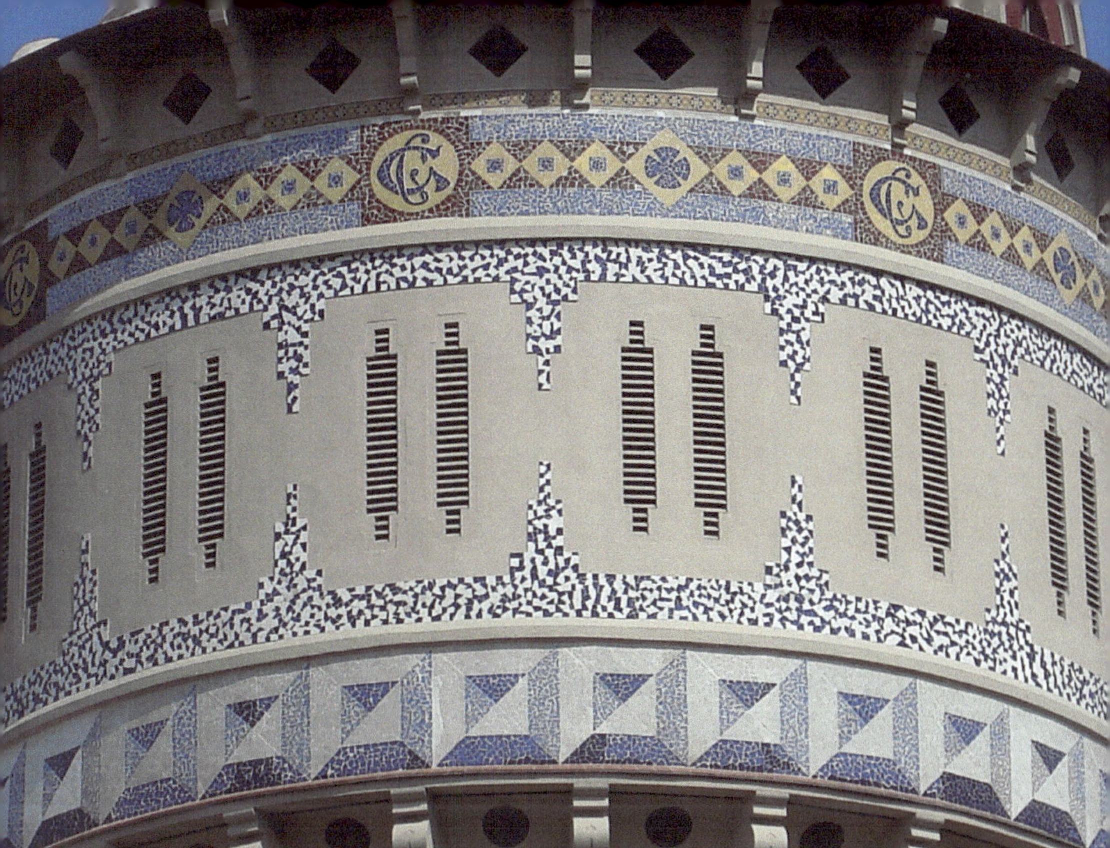

13. The haunted tower

The Torre de les Aigües includes a free ghost story in this guide to free art in Barcelona. Completed in 1907, it is by Josep Domènech i Estapà (1858–1917), commissioned when the company Sociedad Catalana para el Alumbrado de Gas—later Catalana de Gas—expanded its facilities to include a 45-metre-high water tower.

Though active during the years when Modernisme, the Catalan variant of Art Nouveau was evolving, Domènech i Estapà generally rejected the new architecture, even to the extent of penning anti-Modernista treatises. However, he created his own style that was well-accepted in his day and exists comfortably alongside that of other Modernista architects. The octagonal tower displays certain features of

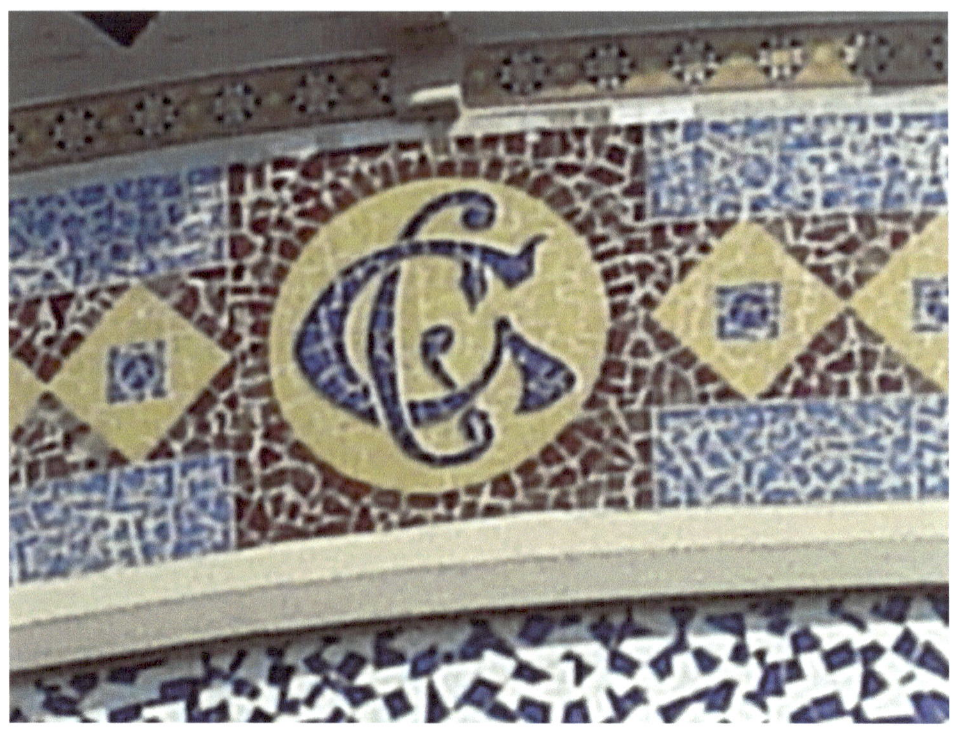

"CG", the Catalana de Gas company monogram,
is depicted in bright ceramic mosaic, adopting
Gaudí's innovation of broken-tile trencadís.

the new architecture such as its turret roof (revealing an Art-Nouveau willingness to fantasise with exotic elements), the exposed brickwork (a very twentieth-century lack of shame for function displayed) and its bright ceramic decoration (even adopting Gaudí's innovation of broken-tile *trencadís* though in a more geometric arrangement). Yet Domènech i Estapà's best efforts to design for a *fin-de-siècle* future nevertheless evince a conservativism that links him to previous styles such as Enlightenment rationalism.

The story goes that, during construction, the architect, lacking the technical skills to design the complex pumping mechanism required, requested the services of a friend, a professor at the Escola Industrial de Barcelona, for its

                          Kevin Booth

design. Pau, one of the school's talented graduates, undertook the project, which lasted two years. When it was finally inaugurated, attended by the top tier of Barcelona society, the pumping station failed to work. Shamed and humiliated, Pau desperately revised the installation over the ensuing days yet, unable to find the error, he finally committed suicide by throwing himself from the top of the tower.

Two weeks afterwards it was discovered that the installation had been designed perfectly. The fault lay in the fact that one of the valves, shipped from Britain—a leading industrial nation—opened in the opposite direction to valves produced in other parts of Europe. A simple reversal was enough to fix the problem.

The turret roof and details such as this round
dormer window reveal an Art-Nouveau willingness
to fantasise with exotic elements.

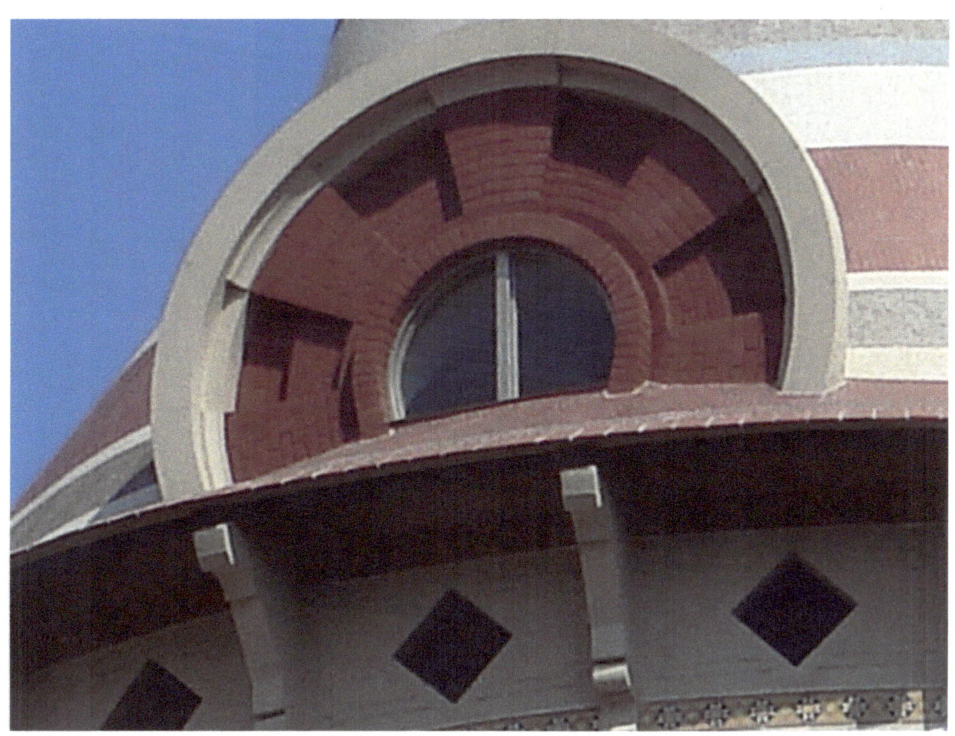

Some say that when traffic is scarce on the nearby ring road and silence claims the park, you can hear somebody working away with a hammer within, rattling his toolbox. Others swear that English visitors to the tower are unable to see its vivid colours, perceiving only greyish hues.

Torre de les aigües de la companyia Catalana de Gas / Catalana de Gas water tower, Josep Domènech i Estapà, 1907. Carrer del Gas, 3, Park de la Barceloneta, Barceloneta.

Coordinates: *41.383779, 2.192561*

References:
http://modernistespuntcom.blogspot.com.es/2010/01/torre-de-les-aigues.html

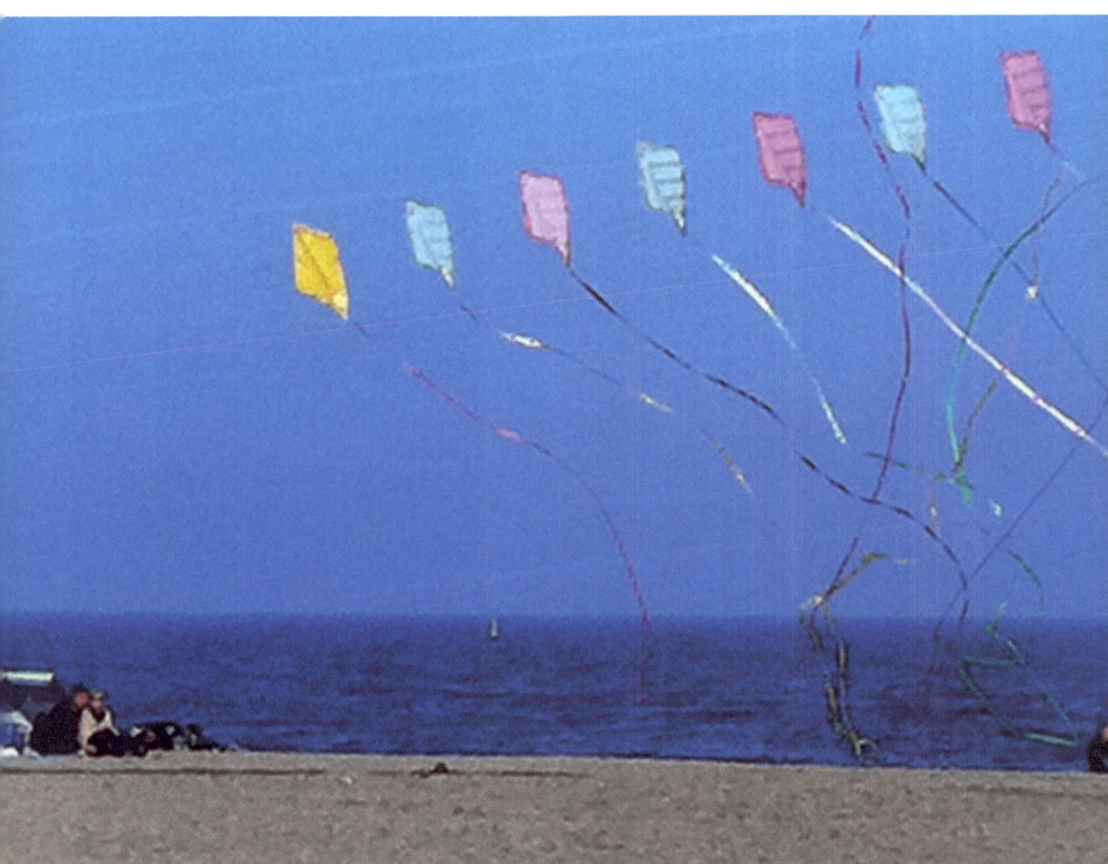

About the author

Born in New Zealand and trained as an actor there and in Australia, Kevin Booth worked in theatre, film and television in Australasia and Spain. He graduated in Literature at the Open University (UK) in 2005, and completed a post-graduate year in Comparative Literature at the University of Auckland (NZ) in 2008. He lives between Barcelona and London, combining work as a translator and editor with writing. You can read about more free art in Barcelona at www.barcelonafreeart.net.

Acknowledgements

I am especially grateful to Maria Friels for her ever-careful proofreading and correction. Any remaining errors, whether of fact or grammar, are my own. I would also like to thank Jordi Padrell, Pau Ferrer, Andreu León, Evan Woodruffe and Nick Lloyd for their encouraging input both into my blog and these guides as they were taking shape.

The translated excerpt of Salvat-Papasseit's poem, "Nocturn per acordió" ("Nocturn for Accordion") is reprinted with kind permission from the translators, Dominic Keown and Tom Owen. You can access the full text and more of his poetry translated at the Anglo-Catalan Society (http://www.anglo-catalan.org/downloads/acsop-monographs/issue02.pdf).

Other books about Barcelona

If you would like to read a novel featuring Barcelona, here are some suggestions:

Celia's Room

by Kevin Booth

"Nothing is quite as it seems. This book rejoices in ambiguity and ambivalence, successfully capturing the zeitgeist of Barcelona."

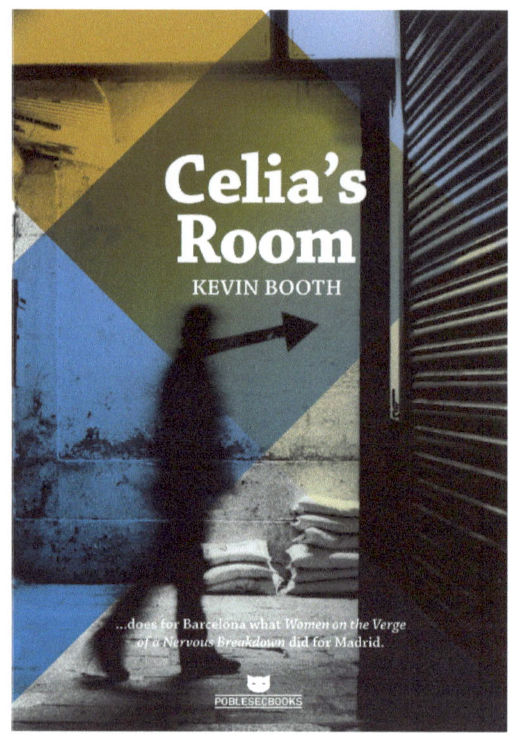

Told through their own eyes, sensitive Joaquim—whose passion for painting will propel him into the artist's life—and cynical Eduardo—addicted to a nightlife that thwarts his ambition to write—unveil a sexual, dreamlike city, personified by the enigmatic Celia. Despite their violently contrasting natures, Joaquim and Eduardo both fall under her aura. The games they are learning to play will draw all three into conflict—against the backdrop of a city that is also rehearsing a new identity—leading them inexorably towards the truth of Celia's Room.

"Stunning debut: If you like Kerouac or Isherwood, you will love Celia's Room."

 Kevin Booth

The Thief's Journal

by Jean Genet
(*Journal du voleur*, Grove Press [1949] 1994). Perhaps Jean Genet's most famous work, a part-fact, part-fiction autobiography that charts the author's progress through Europe in a curiously depoliticised 1930s, wearing nothing but rags and enduring hunger, contempt, fatigue and vice. Spain, Italy, Austria, Czechoslovakia, Poland, Nazi Germany, Belgium... everywhere is the same: bars, dives, flop-houses; robbery, prison and expulsion.

No Word from Gurb

by Eduardo Mendoza
(*Sin noticias de Gurb*, Telegram Books, [1990] 2007). A shape-shifting extraterrestrial named Gurb has assumed the form of Madonna and disappeared in Barcelona's back streets. His hapless commander, desperately trying to find him, records the daily pleasures, dangers, and absurdities of our fragile world while munching his way through enormous quantities of *churros*. No stone is left unturned in the search for Gurb.

The Time of the Doves

by Mercè Rodoreda
(*La plaça del diamant*, Graywolf Press [1962] 1986). This, the author's most famous work, takes place in the Barcelona neighbourhood of Gràcia, before, during and after the Spanish Civil War. Colometa ("Little Dove") is an initially simple neighbourhood girl and young mother who develops through her hardship from a scared, passive soul into a survivor.

Other Poble Sec Books

Celia's Room

"The Jewel Fish Chronicles"

01: Through the Whirlpool

02: Twilight Crosser

03: Lake of Stone

BCN Free Art guides

01: The Port and Barceloneta

02: Montjuïc Mountain

03: The Born and Poble Nou

04: The Ramblas and the Raval

POBLESECBOOKS

www.poblesecbooks.com

 Kevin Booth